THE ILLUSTRATED REFERENCE

ON

CACTI AND OTHER SUCCULENTS

VOLUME TWO

By Edgar Lamb

ILLUSTRATED REFERENCE ON CACTI AND OTHER SUCCULENTS

— Vol. I (1955, 1958, 1963)

— Vol. II (1959, 1968, 1973)
By Edgar and Brian Lamb

— Vol. III (1963, 1971)

— Vol. IV (1966)

— Vol. V (1978)

POCKET ENCYCLOPAEDIA OF CACTI IN COLOUR
INCLUDING OTHER SUCCULENTS (1969)

COLOURFUL CACTI AND OTHER SUCCULENTS OF THE DESERTS (1974)

POPULAR EXOTIC CACTI IN COLOUR (1975)

also

Photographic Reference Plates on Cacti and other Succulents

THE ILLUSTRATED REFERENCE ON

CACTI & OTHER

SUCCULENTS

VOLUME TWO

written and photographed by
EDGAR AND BRIAN LAMB

BLANDFORD PRESS
POOLE   DORSET

First published in 1959

Copyright 1959, 1968, 1973 Blandford Press Limited
Link House, West Street, Poole, Dorset BH15 1LL
2nd Edition 1968
3rd Edition 1973
Reprinted 1978

ISBN 0 7137 0623 6

Set and Printed in Great Britain by Tonbridge Printers Ltd., Tonbridge, Kent.

CONTENTS

ACKNOWLEDGMENT

Special thanks are due to Eric Sventenius for his useful data on Canarian succulents.

COLOUR PLATES

Owing to make-up it has not been possible in every case to place the colour plates in Group sequence

322

BLACK AND WHITE PLATES

Plate Nos. and Page Nos. continue from Volume One

PART ONE: CACTI

PART TWO: SUCCULENTS
OTHER THAN CACTI

PREFACE

Since the first publication of this volume in 1959 the series of illustrated reference books, of which it is a part, has grown to five volumes, with more than 1,300 photographs, of which are 400 are now in colour. Although these four volumes are regarded as something of a complete library, each stands distinctively in its own right.

This volume illustrates such species as the non-South African *Euphorbias*, a number of *Agaves*, and many interesting Canarian succulents, which have rarely been published before. Some may never have been pictured, or perhaps only as a " line drawing ".

The Exotic Collection has, of course, grown extensively in recent years and all photography is done of species in this collection. The work of the Exotic Collection is covered in a separate appendix on p. 571, and for the convenience of our readers we now include in each volume an index to the genera which are covered by the five volumes.

Worthing, England   EDGAR AND BRIAN LAMB*

---

* Since the original publication of this volume Mr. Edgar Lamb's son, Brian Lamb has joined him in " The Exotic Collection " and its more recent publications.

Part One

CACTI

OPUNTIA GROUP

As with Volume I, all three types coming within this group are included in the illustrations. There are the " Cylindric "; the dwarf *Opuntias* with egg-shaped or elongated joints, often known as *Tephrocacti*; and the well-known " flat-jointed " or " Prickly Pear " type.

In addition, three genera coming within this group but not previously illustrated are included.

These are *Maihuenia*, *Quiabentia* and *Pterocactus*, all dwarf or low-growing plants, the first two mentioned being rather similar in growing habit, and without glochids. Both possess leaves which remain on the plants for a long time.

Maihuenia has the distinction of coming from one of the most southerly parts of the world, namely the extreme south of South America. These are hardy, capable of withstanding very severe frost and snow, and are therefore ideal for cold greenhouse or the hardy cactus rockery, in temperate climates.

Quiabentia is not hardy, coming from the warm areas of Brazil and Bolivia, and must therefore be grown accordingly. *Pterocactus*, however, is able to stand indoor cold but cannot be classed as hardy. Very minute glochids are usually found among species in this genus.

All these plants have been growing in this collection for many years, and it can be said that few of those illustrated are too big for the average collector to grow and accommodate. *Opuntia linguiformis* can produce rather long joints and may tend to sprawl, *O. dillenii* may eventually become large but is not so fast-growing, and *O. santarita* requires some years to grow very large.

The remainder can be regarded as mostly small-growing or dwarf, and a proportion can flower in cultivation quite regularly.

Maihuenia poeppigii *Weber*
(Chile)

COLOUR: Green stems, often brownish at base with age. Green leaves and white spines.

SIZE: Natural size shown.

NOTE: This is a very hardy species which can be grown outside in the " Hardy cactus-bed " as it will stand much below freezing, also snow.

In the greenhouse it should have a very rich leafmould soil, a wide pan in which to spread, water at all times of the year (even in cold winter weather), and should be *very freely watered* throughout all summer months.

Not common in collections today, but an easy plant to grow if above notes are observed.

Opuntia cylindrica *D.C.* and
Opuntia cylindrica **fa. cristata** *Hort.*
(Ecuador and Peru)

COLOUR: Stems usually shiny green with nearly white spines.

SIZE: Shown at half size of plant photographed.

NOTE: The above plant has the " cristate " form as well as the normal growing together.

An easy plant to grow, likes a good soil, about average water during all summer months, and slight water in winter if in a warmed greenhouse.

Grown indoors near a window, slight water in winter may be essential.

330

Opuntia leptocaulis *D.C.*
(Mexico)

COLOUR: Dull green or yellowish-green with yellow-straw coloured spines.

SIZE: Natural size shown above.

NOTE: Popular in collections and often used in table-gardens, also indoors.

Normal soils, water and general culture. This species stands dry cold very well.

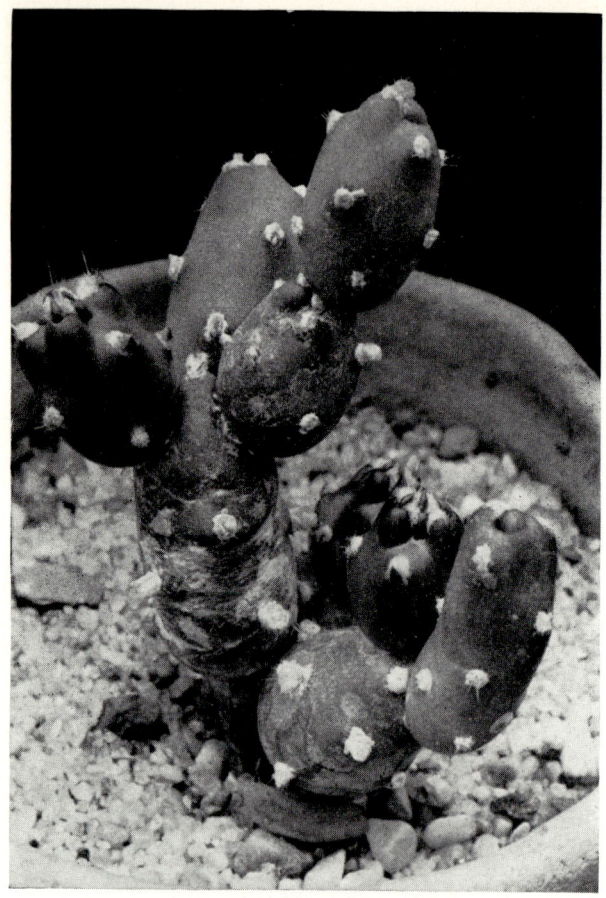

Opuntia subinermis *Bckbg.*
(Argentina?)

COLOUR: Pale or dull green pads or joints, sometimes yellowish and having off-white glochids and very short spines if present.

SIZE: Shown at double natural size.

NOTE: Not a fast growing species. Requires less water than average at all times.

Normal soil, but rather special care in drainage is advised. Grown indoors, the joints tend to " elongate " rather more than is natural.

332

Opuntia dillenii *Haw.*
(W. Indies)

COLOUR: Green or yellow-green pads with golden-yellow spines.

SIZE: Shown at approximately half-size of part of plant photographed.

NOTE: Forms of this species are widely distributed throughout the succulent world. The plant shown above is the Canary Isles form which is very well known, although this has become established here, and is not native to the Canary Isles.

Will stand winter cold well, likes plenty of water and a very rich soil when its spines will develop fully.

Opuntia erinacea *Engelm.*
(S.W. U.S.A.)

COLOUR: Pads almost entirely hidden with white spines.

SIZE: Shown at about half-size.

NOTE: A slower growing *Opuntia*, capable of standing dry cold very well. In summer water rather less than average except in very hot weather.

Opuntia linguiformis *Griffiths*
(Texas)

COLOUR: Bright green or yellow-green pads with pale yellow spines.

SIZE: Varying considerably in length, the above shows end of one
              elongated pad at half-size.

NOTE: Producing very long " tongue-like " pads. Not so large if grown
in pots, however.
Will stand winter cold well if dry. In all growing months, plenty of water
Not very suited to indoor culture because of size.

Opuntia microdasys *Pfeiffer*
(Mexico)

COLOUR: Golden yellow glochids, on a dull green plant.

SIZE: The plant pictured is shown very slightly enlarged.

NOTE: A popular species for greenhouse or indoor growing. Normal water and soil but slight winter warmth is advised.

Forms a well-branched plant in a year or two of growing.

Opuntia santa-rita *Rose*
(Arizona)

COLOUR: Pads very colourful—blue to reddish with deeper colouring at areoles often in streaks. Spines few—red-brown to blackish.

SIZE: Shown at slightly under half size.

NOTE: An attractive species, the colour being most striking. At the areole positions, colours give the appearance of having " run ".

A feature of this species is the few oddly placed spines which are not usually found on newest pads; these are mostly twisted.

Normal water, soil, etc., suits this plant.

Pterocactus kuntzei *K. Sch.*
(Argentina and Patagonia)

COLOUR: Body of plants usually bronzed, spines are white, many of these almost flattened against the plant.

SIZE: Shown very slightly enlarged.

NOTE: Average water in summer, and slight watering during winter months but only in the warmed greenhouse. It will stand cold and dry but stems sometimes wither from the tips if allowed to be dry for too long.

This tuberous rooted plant will re-grow even if it has lost all its stems due to drought.

Quiabentia chacoensis *Bckbg.*
(Brazil and Bolivia)

COLOUR: Usually yellow-green, leaves green when present, spines white.

SIZE: Natural size shown above.

NOTE: Quite rare in many collections today, yet not difficult to grow. Requires some warmth in winter.

A rich leafmould soil and average water throughout all growing months is suitable for this interesting species, with its horizontal branches and strange growing form.

CEREUS GROUP

In this large and variable group of cacti, I have included seven additional genera which did not appear in Volume I as illustrations, namely: *Borzicactus, Carnegiea, Eulychnia, Lemaireocereus, Machaerocereus, Selenicereus* and *Stetsonia*.

Borzicacti are usually of slender growth, erect or inclined to sprawl when stems are long, their flowers in many ways resembling those of the *Cleistocacti*, except that they open wider.

Carnegiea is a monotypic genus, known also as " The Saguaro ", very slow-growing but with age attaining great heights.

Eulychnia is capable of standing dry cold, but cannot be regarded as completely hardy as in nature it is found in very dry habitats. All species are very spiny, some spines as long as 7 in. (17·8 cm) or even more.

Lemaireocereus coming from warmer climates need some winter protection, most being included to develop a " blue " colouring on their stems and not flowering as small plants.

Machaerocereus contains two species, the one illustrated being of erect habit, freely branched with age.

Selenicereus is night-flowering, but very beautiful. The species illustrated is easily identified by its raised tubercles from which a few spines grow.

Stetsonia flowering only on old plants, slow-growing and very spiny, is always regarded as a very attractive plant in the young stage.

Among the colour illustrations I have included several *Echinocerei*, showing their beautiful flowers and forms. Note such species as *E. fendleri, E. baileyi*, etc., where considerable variation occurs with both plant and flower.

Carnegiea gigantea *B. & R.*
(Arizona)

COLOUR: Body of plant dull to almost grey-green. Spines grey with
age but whilst in growth, spines on top being red.

SIZE: Top of a 3-ft. (91·5 cm) tall specimen, measuring about
7–8 in. (17·8 cm–20·3 cm) in diameter.

NOTE: Slow growing, this plant is rare in collections other than as small
seedlings or young plants.
Growing period of adult plants is even more limited than with seedlings,
extending usually only over the months of June and July.
Water freely when growing, lightly at other times except in winter when the
plant should be quite dry. A wide pot or pan is advisable as roots spread
considerably.

Cereus peruvianus fa. monstrosus *De Cand.*
(Uncertain)

COLOUR: Dull green or grey-green, particularly on older parts of stems. Spines variable, often yellow-greyish.

SIZE: The part of plant photographed is shown at about one-third actual size.

NOTE: An easy species to grow, whether small or large. Give water freely throughout all growing months. Keep dry in coldest winter months, when it will stand dry cold quite well.

A rich leafmould soil gives best results but will grow quite well in almost any soil and under very different conditions. Popular indoors also.

Shapes vary a great deal, but whether as a young seedling or a giant specimen, these curious formations are present. Large specimens flower well.

Cereus variabilis *Pfeiff.*
(Brazil)

COLOUR: Green stems, often pale with white areoles and dark brown spines.

SIZE: Widest part of this plant measures 5 in. (12·7 cm) across.

NOTE: The flower is large white, greenish inside on a long tube; the fruits are quite spectacular as can be seen in the colour illustration on page 345.

Stands dry winter cold very well, likes a rich soil and plenty of water during all growing months.

This is a night flowering species. Flowers usually begin to open in the evening and close the following morning. Very fragrant.

Top
XXXIII
Borzicactus sepium *B. & R.*
(Ecuador)

These species belong to the CEREUS GROUP

NOTE: While this plant will stand the dry cold greenhouse, slightly warmer temperatures are advised.

Hairy buds sometimes form on the plant in autumn and remain until spring before actually flowering. Note the " spiral " hair formation of one of the buds.

Flowers when fully extended project 2–2½ in. (5–6·3 cm) from the plant.

Bottom
XXXIV
Cereus variabilis *Pfeiff.*
(Brazil)

NOTE: This plant, as its name implies, is very variable in form but has the usual large flower projecting some 8–9 in. (20·3–22·8 cm) and about 4 in. (10·2 cm) in diameter when expanded. Flowers open during early evening and close during the following morning. These are very fragrant and fill the greenhouse with their perfume.

An easy plant to grow, likes much water when in growth but will stand long dry cold in winter, without any water.

Fruits may expand as much as 3 in. (7·6 cm) in diameter; these are also very fragrant.

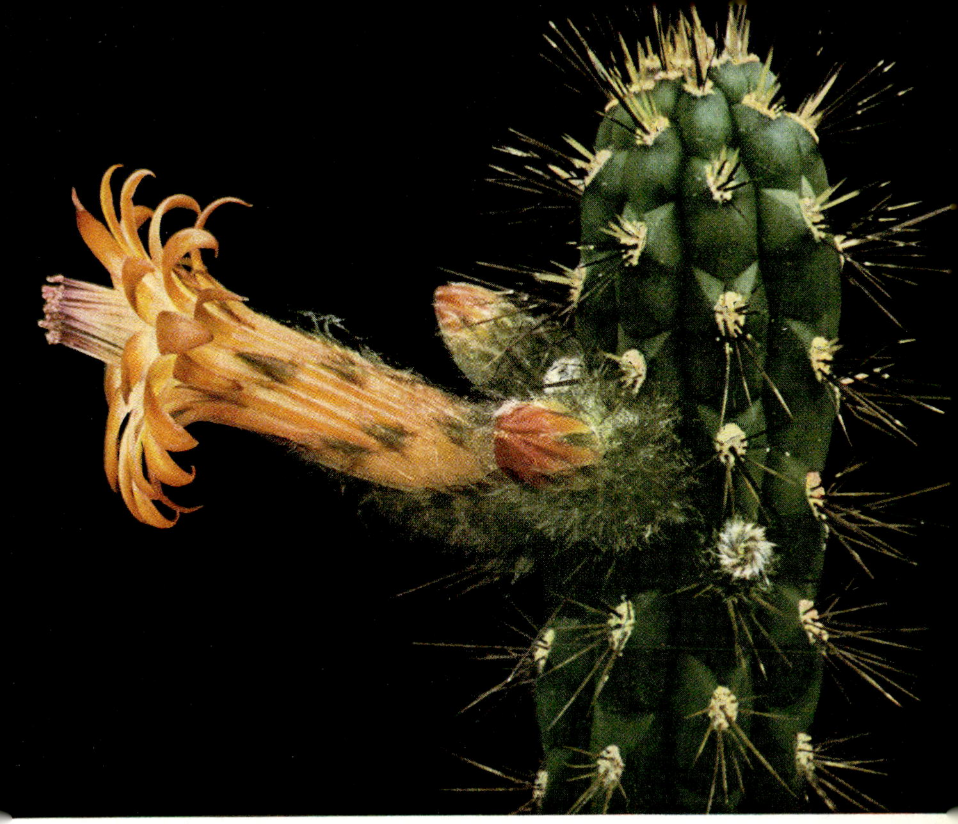

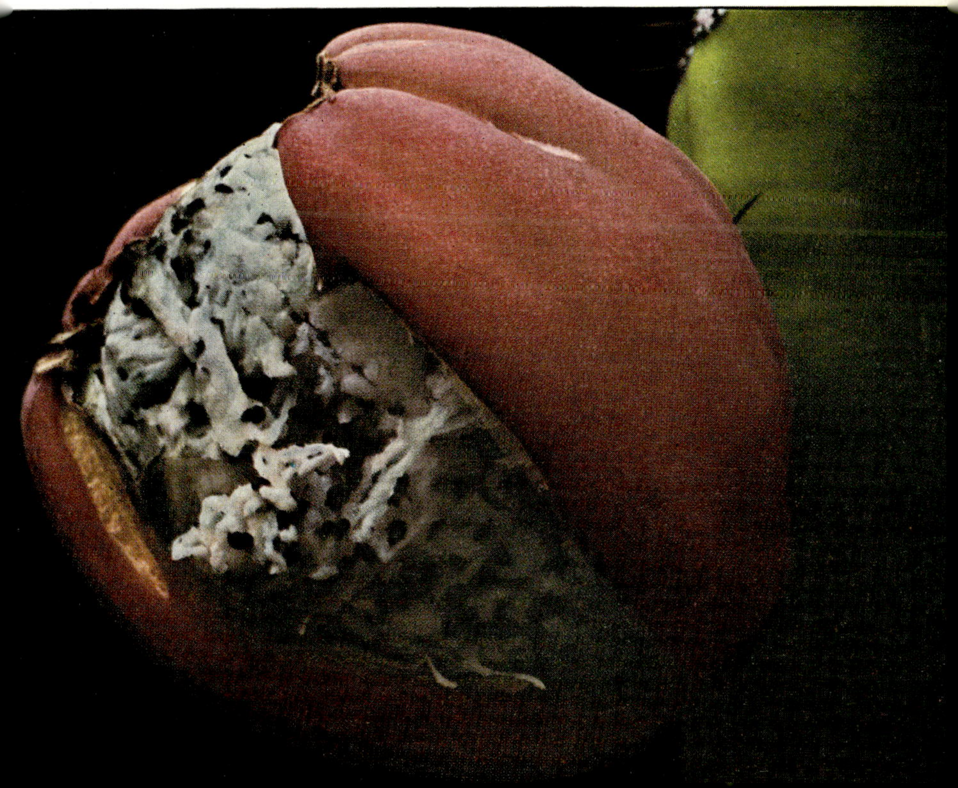

XXXV   *These species belong to the* CEREUS GROUP

Echinocereus fendleri *Engelm.*
(New Mexico)

NOTE: Very variable in spine and flower form, producing its magnificent blooms in May or June.

If quite dry in winter, this plant stands temperatures below freezing without harm. During the growing season, water fairly freely, but a dry cold resting period is essential for good flowering.

Flower size may vary from 2 in. (5 cm) to over 3 in. (7·6 cm) across.

XXXVl

Echinocereus albispinus *Lahm.*
(Oklahoma)

NOTE: Slow growing and requires very good drainage, with rather less water than average at all times.

Stands cold quite well if very dry and is also among those which vary considerably in form, some being so thickly covered in spines as to hide the body of the plant.

Flowers are very beautiful and often exceed 4 in. (10·2 cm) in diameter.

Echinocereus dasyacanthus *Engelm.*
(Texas)

COLOUR: Pale green body, white spines, brown-tipped.

SIZE: Half natural size shown above.

FLOWER: See page 364.

NOTE: One of the most beautiful, as both plant and flower are so attractive. Slow growing and requiring rather less water than average. A long and dry winter resting period assists flowering the following season. Flowers often remain open 2–3 weeks, very large often as much as 5 in. (12·7 cm) when fully open in hot conditions.

This species frequently has flowers of differing colour and not always constant on the same plant. Shown here with fruit.

Echinocereus purpureus *Lahm.*
(Oklahoma)

COLOUR: Whitish brown spines with purple tips, rather obscuring the deep green body colour.

SIZE: Actual size shown.

FLOWER: Deep magenta with green centre.

NOTE: Slow growing and producing spectacular flowers, shown above just opening.

Rarely branching, this species likes a good soil with leafmould, rather less than average water, dry in winter when it will stand cold well.

Eulychnia spinibarbis *Otto.*

(Chile)

COLOUR: Pale green plant, grey-white areoles and spines. Newest spines at tips are brown.

SIZE: Half actual size shown.

NOTE: A very long-spined species, rare in most collections today. Will stand dry winter cold well, is a slow grower and requires extra care in drainage; rather less than normal water, except in very hot weather.

Lemaireocereus chichipe *B. & R.*
(Mexico)

COLOUR: Usually light green, with whitish spines, tipped dark brown or nearly black.

SIZE: Top of plant photographed is shown slightly enlarged.

NOTE: A strong, rather sturdy plant which will grow in most soils. With average water in summer, dry in winter, this species is not difficult in any way. Not a fast grower for the type of plant.

351

Lemaireocereus thurberi *B. & R.*
(Mexico)

COLOUR: Grey-green or even bronzed with very dark brown or near black areoles and greyish spines, tipped darker.

SIZE: The plant pictured is shown slightly enlarged.

NOTE: A very slow grower, requires normal watering and a well-drained soil. Dry in winter, it will stand cold.

Not very suited to indoor culture.

Machaerocereus gummosus *Engelm.*
(Lower California)

COLOUR: Often the green is much bronzed. The plant has white
areoles, grey spines, some being dark brown or blackish.

SIZE:　　　Actual size of plant pictured.

NOTE: A slow grower, requiring good drainage and rather less than
average water, none in winter when normal dry cold does no harm.

Not very suited to indoor culture.

Selenicereus macdonaldiae *B. & R.*
(Argentina)

COLOUR: Stems light green in colour and with whitish spines.

SIZE: Tip of growing stem shown about natural size.

NOTE: Among the well-known night-flowering species, stem may trail or clamber to great lengths. Flowers very large, fragrant and produced at almost any positions along the stems.

With a rich leafmould soil, plenty of water in all warm months, and slight winter warmth when a little water may be given, this plant will do well. Branching at various points on the stems, fairly fast growing.

354

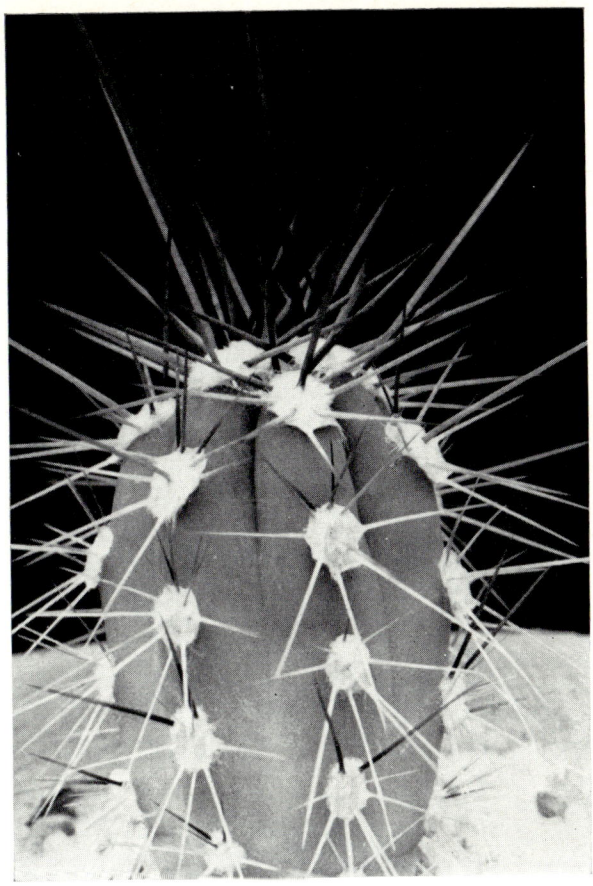

Stetsonia coryne *B. & R.*
(N.W. Argentina)

COLOUR: Green, often grey-green with white areoles and white spines as shown, the near black spines being on the upper parts of areoles.

SIZE: This fairly young plant is shown slightly enlarged.

NOTE: Not a fast growing species yet not at all difficult. It will stand winter cold well if quite dry.

Water about average in summer months, best grown in a fairly rich soil, these plants, particularly when young, are very handsome.

355

PILOCEREUS GROUP

Most of the plants in this group are among the finest for attractive form, despite the fact that the majority do not flower until quite large. Their hairy nature varies from a coarse hair as in *Cephalocereus* and *Oreocereus* to the very fine, silky covering on *Espostoas*.

Espostoa adds one more genus to be illustrated as an extra to Volume I. *Espostoa melanostele* used to be known as " *Pseudoespostoa* " but has been returned to the position now given.

Oreocerei grown from seed over the years have been observed to produce a proportion of young plants completely without hair, in some cases the hair forming on top after a few years, but not in all instances.

None of this group can be considered as fast-growing, some being very slow, but even as young plants they can be recognised as being " miniatures " of the large specimens.

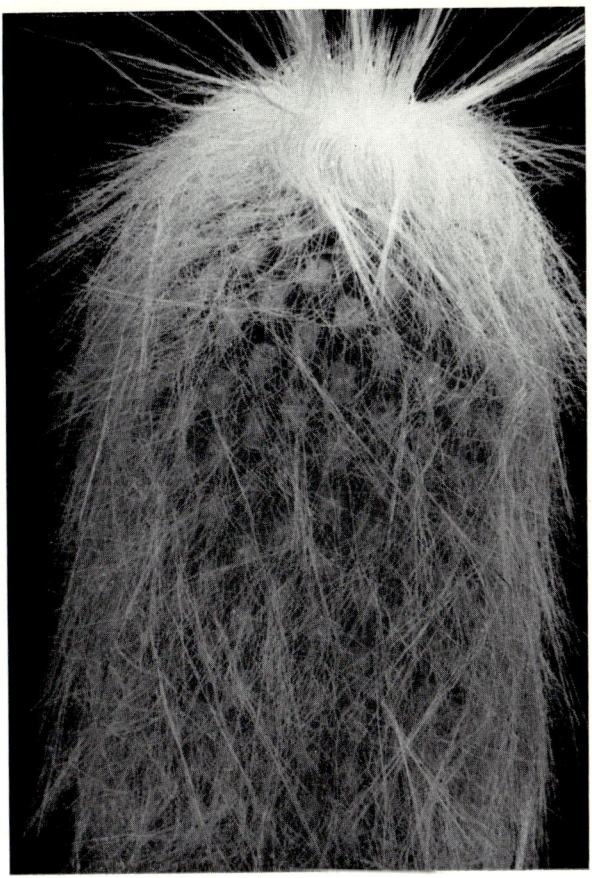

Cephalocereus senilis *Pfeiff.*
(Mexico)

COLOUR: Body of plant almost completely hidden with long trailing white hair, through which some spines protrude.

SIZE: Top of a 3-ft. (91·5 cm) specimen shown at about half-normal size.

NOTE: Popular species, even young seedlings can be completely covered with the long white hair.

Requires rather less water than many, extra care in drainage is important.

Will stand dry cold in winter, but young growing plants are better with very slight warmth.

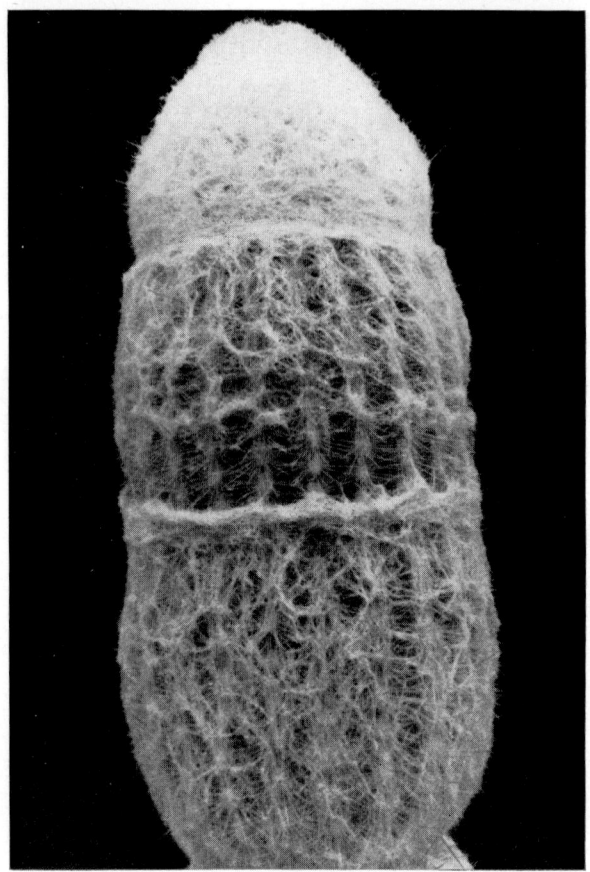

Espostoa lanata *B. & R.*
(Ecuador)

COLOUR: Green but almost covered with white silky-hair, some sharp spines being present.

SIZE: Top of plant photographed is shown slightly reduced.

NOTE: Slow growing and requiring very sandy soil, rather less water than average and cold dry winter position.

Care should always be taken to ensure good drainage, otherwise the roots may rot.

Not very suited to indoor culture.

Espostoa melanostele *Borg.*
(Peru)

COLOUR: Covered with very fine, silky white hair; some thin " needle-like " spines, pale yellow or pink tinted may protrude.

SIZE: Slightly enlarged illustration of a young plant. Grown from seed in four years.

NOTE: Handsome plants, particularly when young and covered with the silky hair. Older plants tend to lose some of the hair on lower parts, particularly if in poor soil.

Dry cold in winter does no harm. Throughout growing months, water about average, a rich soil giving best results.

Oreocereus celsianus *Ricc.*
(Bolivia)

COLOUR: Body almost covered with coarse hair and with many strong, stout spines, reddish in colour.

SIZE: Top of a tall specimen which measures about 5 in. (12·7cm) across.

NOTE: A slow grower, will stand dry winter cold, even below freezing will do no harm.

Water very freely in summer months and give a fairly rich soil, well drained.

Young plants or seedlings look exactly like the bigger plants and are easy to grow in most average collections; even in the light window they can do quite well, but hair is not always so well developed.

Oreocereus fossulatus *Bckbg.*
(Bolivia and Peru)

COLOUR: Dull green with much white hair, areoles and strong spines being whitish to straw-coloured.

SIZE: A young plant five years from seed is shown at approximately twice actual size.

NOTE: An easy, strong growing plant, capable of standing very cold but dry winter conditions.

Water about average in summer, good drainage and a rich soil being important.

XXXVII

These species belong to the CEREUS GROUP

Echinocereus baileyi *Rose.*

(Oklahoma)

NOTE: Two forms are shown and many others exist but flowers are as usual among the truly beautiful, around 3 in (7·6 cm) in diameter.

Dry cold does not harm this plant, even below freezing in the English climate does no harm so long as the plant is really dry.

An easy growing species, readily raised from seed.

XXXVIII

Echinocereus enneacanthus *Engelm.*

(Mexico)

NOTE: An easy species to grow, requires a fair amount of water when in growth, little in autumn and none at all during the winter when it may tend to shrivel, in which state it can withstand considerable dry cold.

Flowers very large, usually 4 in. (10·2 cm) across.

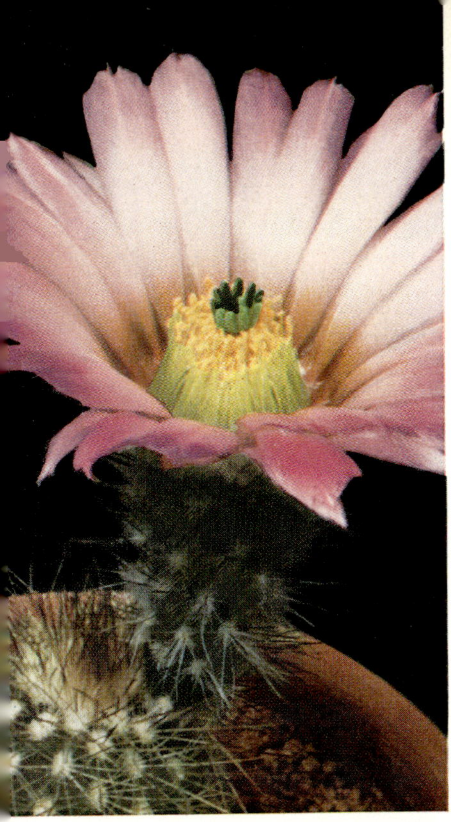
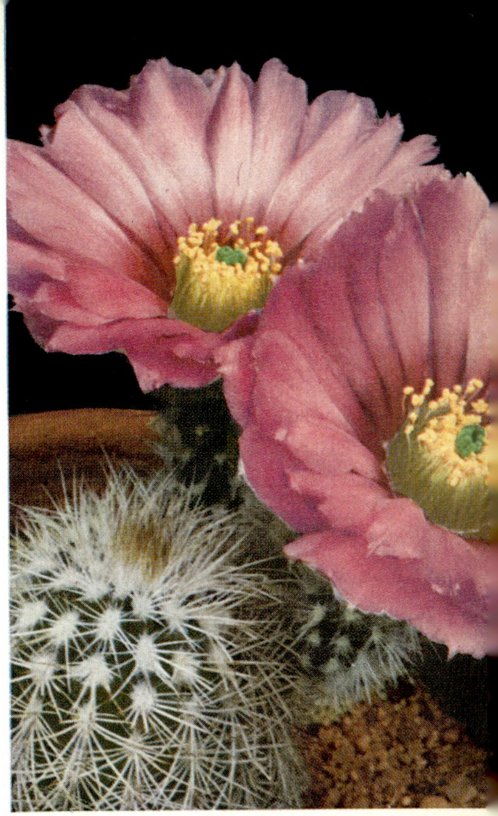
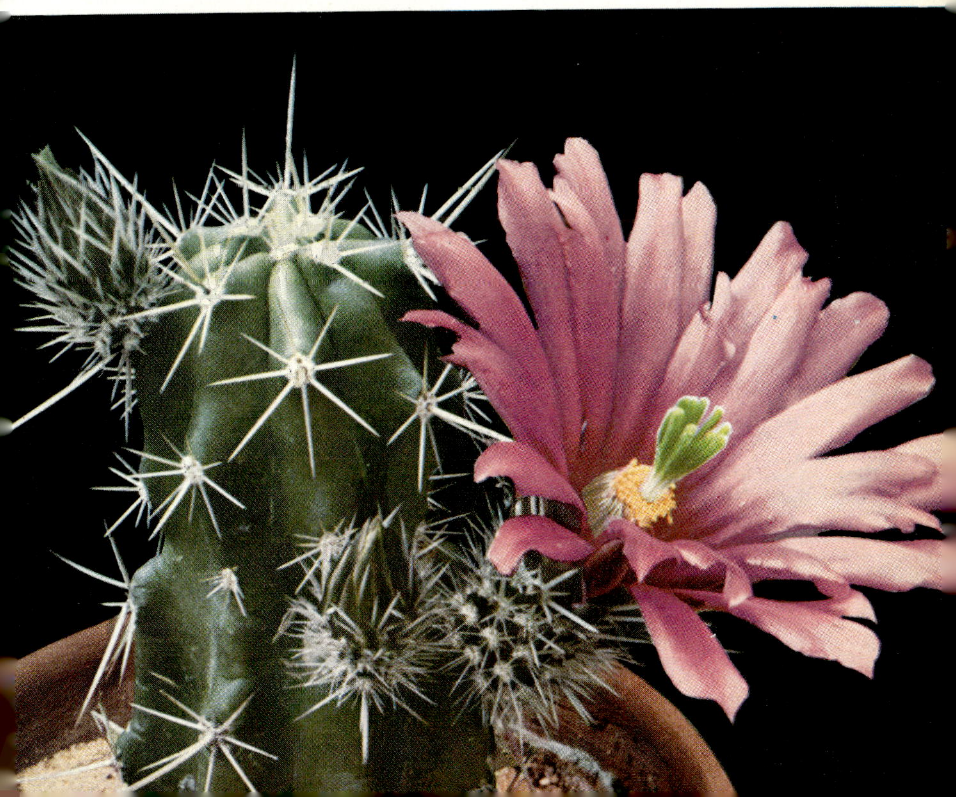

Echinocereus viridiflorus *Engelm.*

(New Mexico)

NOTE: Probably the most variable in form, size and flower. Some are fragrant with a strong scent of " Citrus ", others are without any scent.

All forms are hardy if dry, some being very dwarf, yet flowering on minute plants from several positions at one time.

Good drainage, rather less water than average as plants are slow-growing.

Echinocereus dasyacanthus *Engelm.*

(Texas)

See page 348 for Notes on this species.

Top left
XLI
Lobivia famatimensis var. haematantha *Werd.*
(N. Argentina)

These species belong to the ECHINOPSIS GROUP.

NOTE: Plants grown from seed may well bloom in their third year Plenty of water while in growth, likes leafmould in soil mixture. Flower about 2 in. (5 cm) across.

Top right
XLII
Lobivia pseudocachensis var. salynii *Bckbg.*

NOTE: Slow growing species, requires rather less water than some, but does well in a leafmould soil. Flowers well on small plants, the one pictured being little over 1 in. *(2·54 cm)* across.

Bottom left
XLIII

Lobivia rubescens *Bckbg.*
(Bolivia-Argentina)

See page 371 for Notes on this species.

Bottom right
XLIV

Lobivia wrightiana *Bckbg.*
(Peru)

NOTE: Soil as for other *Lobivias*, water about average or rather extra in growing season—leafmould should be included in soil mixture. Flower tube about 2½–3 in. (6·3–7·6 cm) long.

Some forms of this plant have a single central spine.

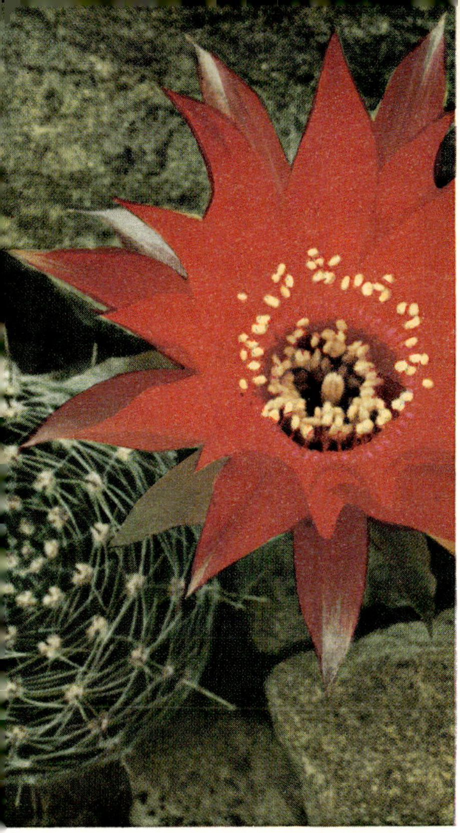
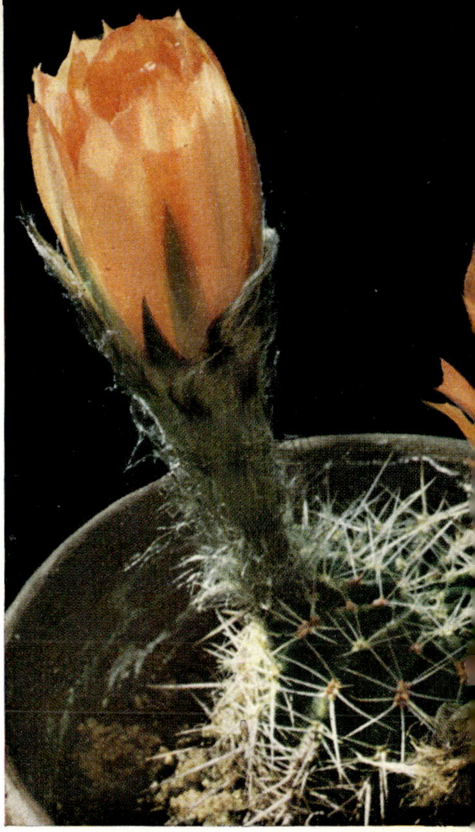
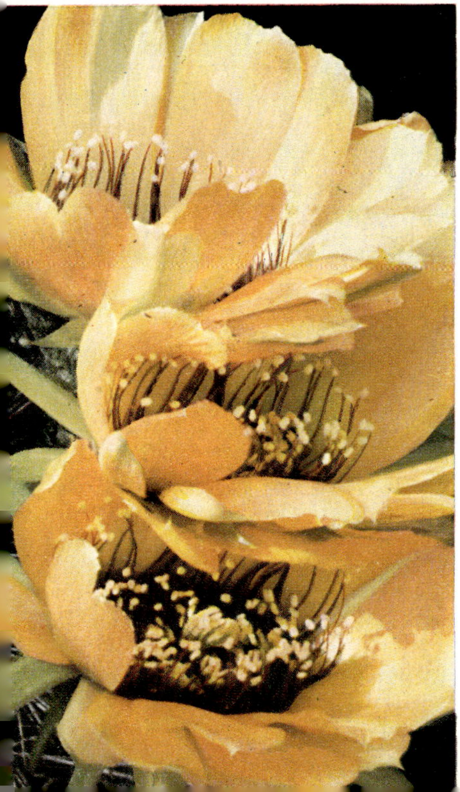
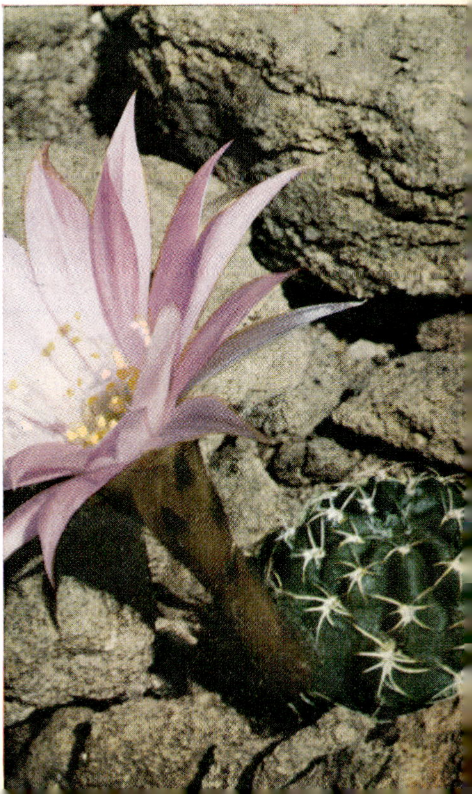

These species belong to the ECHINOPSIS GROUP

Rebutia deminuta *Berger.*
(Argentina)

NOTE: One of the very free-flowering *Rebutias,* as this picture indicates. Plants 1–1½ in. (2·54–3·8 cm) in diameter producing up to 30 or more flowers.

Rebutia krainziana *Kslring.*
(Argentina)

NOTE: Plants about 1 in. (2·54 cm) diameter, or even under, may be expected to bloom each year. (Now often known as *R. calliantha* var. *krainziana.*)

Rebutia senilis var. lilacino-rosea *Bckbg.*
(Argentina)

NOTE: Plants often slightly larger than many other *Rebutias,* very free-flowering—these being about 1 in. (2·54 cm) or just under in size.

Rebutia violaciflora *Bckbg.*
(Argentina)

NOTE: An interesting feature of this beautiful species is the fact that after the flower has opened it increases in diameter for a day or so, as can be seen in the picture. Flower size about average or slightly larger.

A leafmould soil, plenty of water and shaded from direct sunlight will give the finest results with these four species. Keep dry from around mid-December to early March, when flower buds may be noted. (Now often known as *R. minuscula* fa. *violaciflora.*)

ECHINOPSIS GROUP

Plants within this group are noted for their very free-flowering habit, in particular *Rebutias* and *Lobivias*.

As most of these can be regarded as dwarf plants, or small-growing, they are naturally very popular among collectors with a very limited space.

To illustrate the flowering qualities to the full, eight species have been included in the colour photography from which the reader will see just why they are so popular.

It might be stressed here that *all* of the plants illustrated do best with slight shading from direct hot sunlight, plants grow better and the flowering qualities have been found to be much improved.

From many years' experience of growing these fascinating little cacti, leafmould in the soil mixture has been found essential to obtain the desired results. It must be remembered that they cannot be regarded as " desert " cacti, as in nature they thrive among grasses and other leafy protection, thus their natural soil contains " leaf-mould " formed over the years.

Lobivia rubescens *Bckbg.*
(Bolivia-Argentina)

COLOUR: Dark green body, spines on upper half of plant being a rich red-brown, older spines pinkish-grey. Creamy white wool in areoles.

SIZE: Actual size of plant shown.

FLOWER: See page 367.

NOTE: Slow growing and requiring to be a fair size before flowering Normal growing conditions suit this plant which is not difficult.
One special feature of this species is the shape of buds and flowers, these being oval, noted particularly with the buds. Flowers have a deep red throat formed by the filaments being joined together as can be seen in the colour photograph.

ECHINOCACTUS GROUP

This group contains a very wide variety of types, sizes and slow-growing and rarer species, among the latter being such genera as *Ariocarpus*, *Aztekium*, etc.

Eight genera not previously illustrated in Volume I are included here: *Aztekium*, *Echinomastus*, *Eriosyce*, *Hamatocactus*, *Homalocephala*, *Stenocactus* (*Echinofossulocactus*), *Strombocactus* and *Toumeya*.

Aztekium is a very slow-growing rarity but can be flowered easily.

Echinomastus may vary in the plant form, but all are slow-growing species, requiring more care in every way.

Eriosyce are very slow of growth, but with great age they do in nature form into large single heads, comparable in size to the well-known " *Echinocactus grusonii* ".

Hamatocactus is a free-flowering cactus of easy culture.

Homalocephala is a monotypic Genus, renowned for its " fringed " flowers and long-lasting brilliantly-coloured fruits (see colour photograph).

Stenocactus usually recognised by the wavy ribs. Plants within this genus can also be under the genus name of *Echinofossulocactus*, the former having been adopted many years ago as a simpler word, though not strictly correct.

Strombocactus and *Toumeya* are closely allied genera, having much in common. Plants in this genus are somewhat rare in collections today. Both flower in cultivation and are not difficult.

Amongst the half-tone photographs I have included two illustrations of free-flowering *Gymnocalyciums* of dwarf habit, along with two more of this genus in colour.

Ariocarpus fissuratus *K. Sch.*
(Mexico)

COLOUR: Slate grey to greenish with white wool in all fissures of the plant. Upper surface of each tubercle often " chalky " in appearance.

SIZE: Actual size shown above.

NOTE: Flowers in summer may be produced if the plant is kept in a hot sunny position; these are pinkish.

Very little water needed at any time and only in summer weather. Gypsum added to the soil for any plant in this genus is an advantage as it assists flowering.

Ariocarpus furfuraceus *Thompson*
(Mexico)

COLOUR: Pink to grey with much white wool, also a white areole near tip of each tubercle.

SIZE: Actual size shown of plant photographed.

NOTE: Very slow growing, a hot sunny position and very little water at any time.

Open soil essential.

Ariocarpus trigonus *K. Sch.*
(Mexico)

COLOUR: Grey or even grey-olive green with much white wool, a white woolly areole near tip of each tubercle. Older tubercles brown.

SIZE: Actual size shown.

NOTE: Among the slowest growing cacti, a very open soil is essential to allow water to flow away quickly. Hot sunny position when flowers may appear at almost any time, yellowish in colour.

Water very sparsely at all times, none in winter; cold when dry does not appear to do harm.

Ariocarpus retusus *Scheidw.*
(Mexico)

NOTE: Very slow growing species requiring open sandy soil and less than average water at all times.

A long dry resting period in winter is essential. This species will stand hot sunny conditions in summer when its flowers are produced, these being about 1 in. diameter.

Strombocactus disciformis *B. & R.*
(Mexico)

NOTE: Cultivation as above. Flowers often produced during late summer and at times in early spring also, giving two flowering periods in one year.

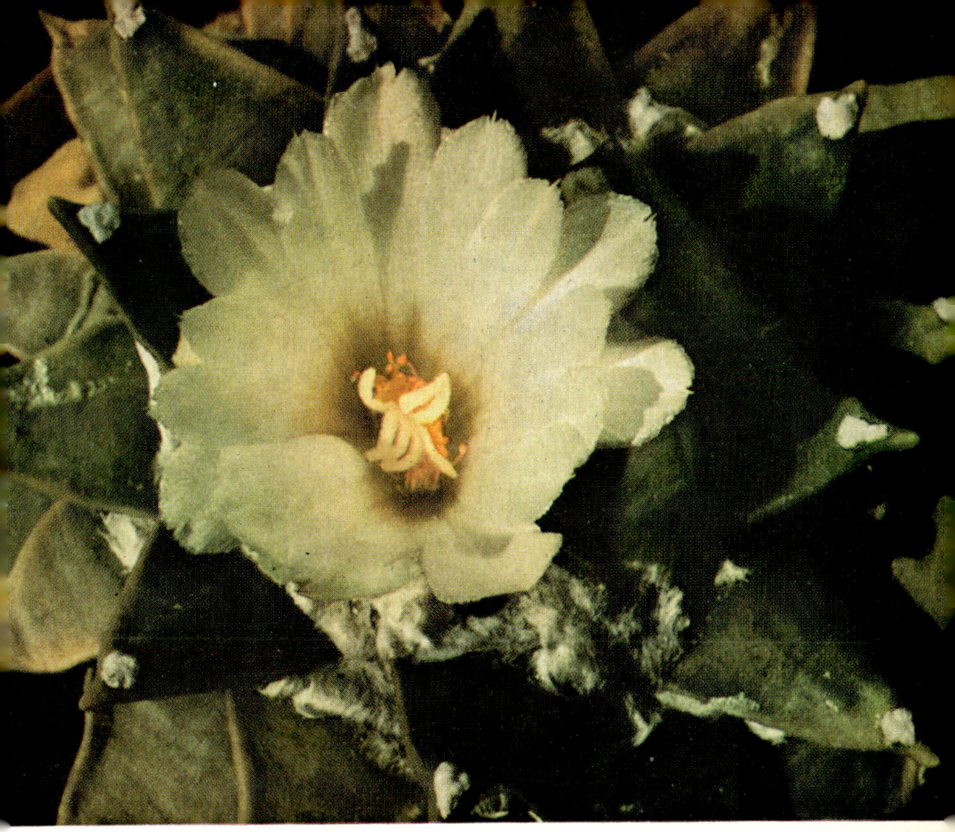

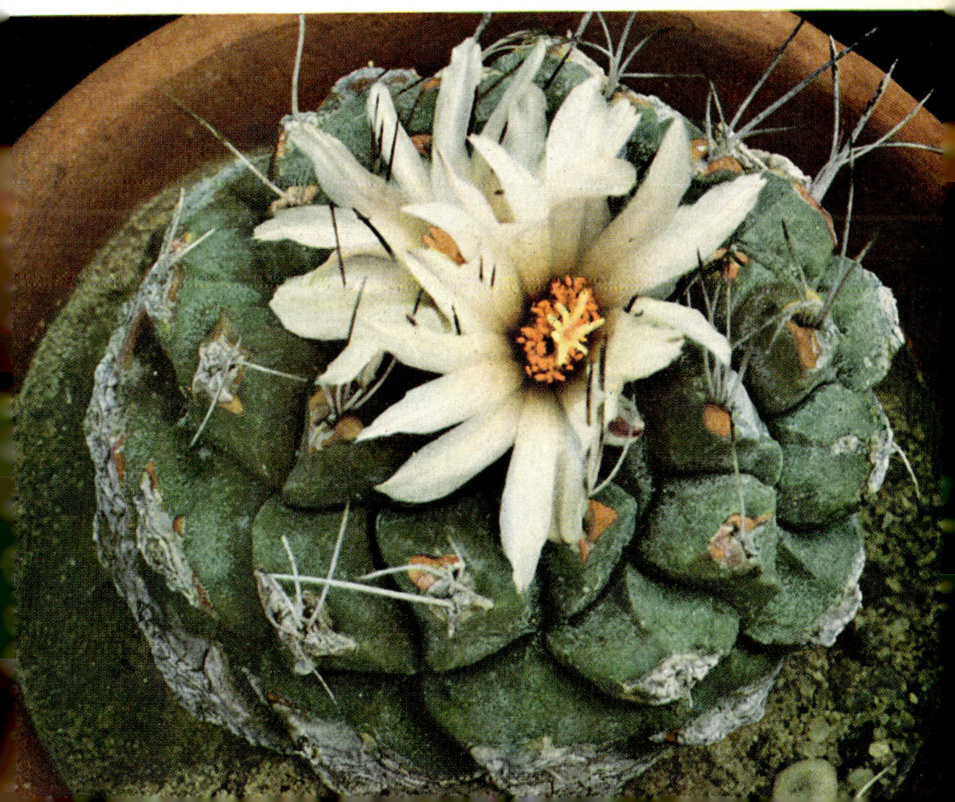

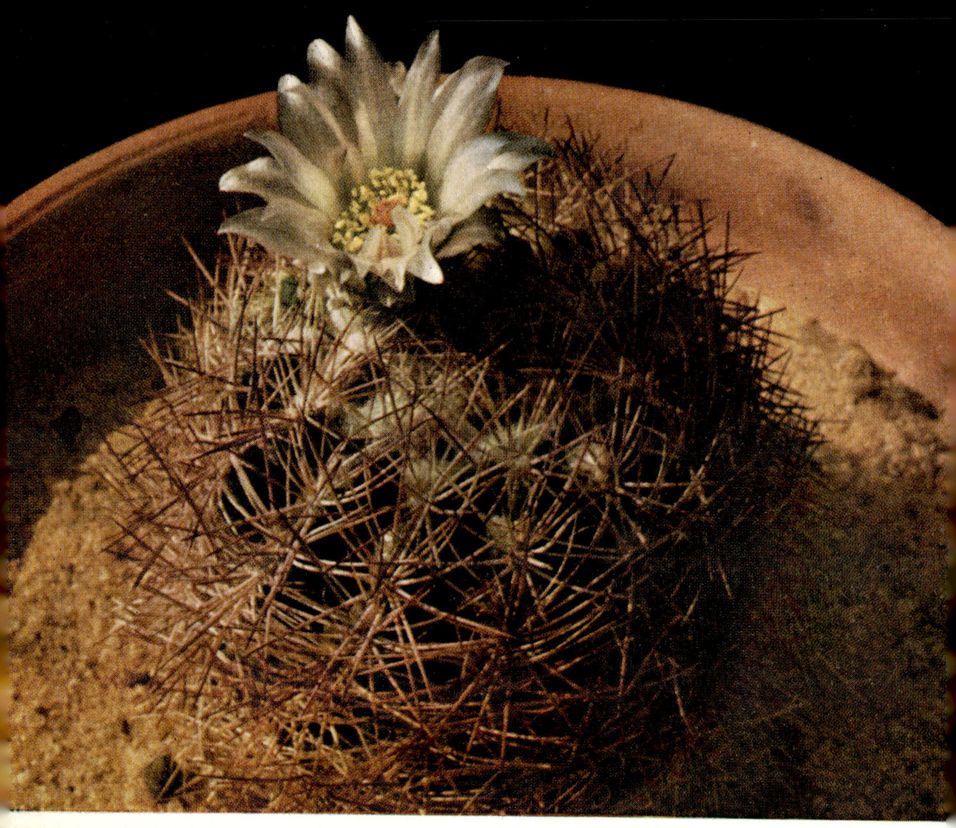

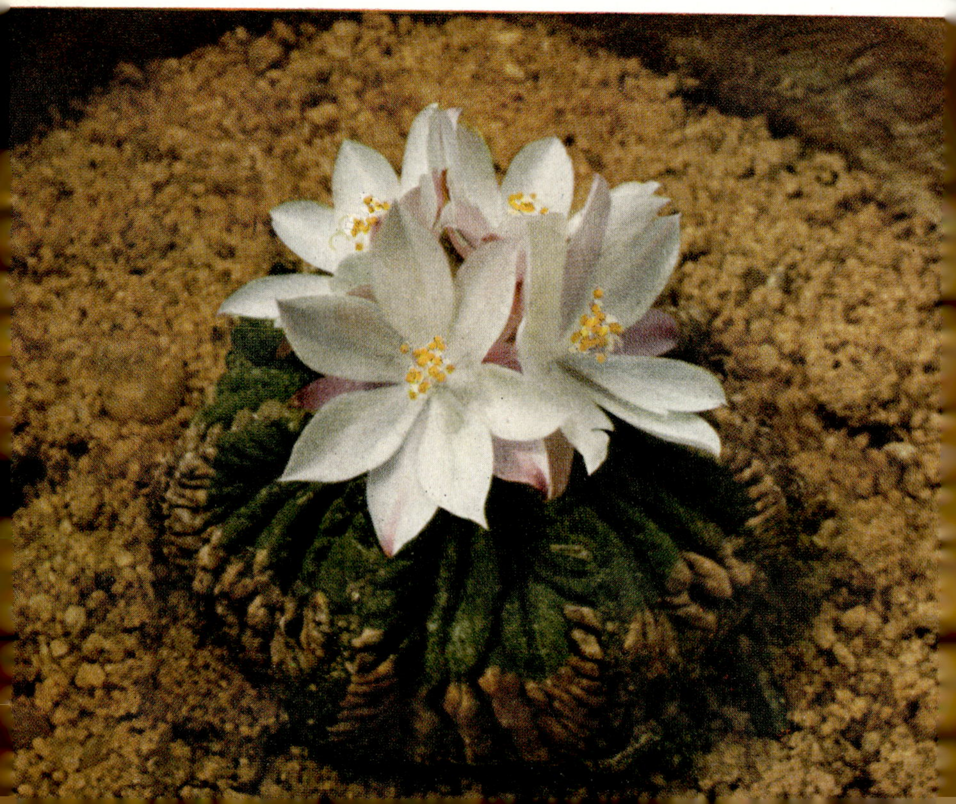

These species belong to the ECHINOCACTUS GROUP

Echinomastus intertextus *Engelm.*
(S.W. U.S.A.)

NOTE: Likes a sandy soil with leafmould but much less water than average at all times. Flowers often unable to open fully due to the dense spine formation.

Slight warmth in winter essential. The plant pictured is growing in a 4-in. (10·2 cm) pan.

Aztekium ritteri *Boed.*
(Mexico)

NOTE: Very slow growing, likes a long dry winter resting period—some gypsum in the soil is considered to be helpful to flowering.

Water lightly at all times, except when flowering and during hot summer weather; pay special attention to good drainage.

Old specimens tend to branch at soil level but these take a long time to develop.

Eriosyce ceratistes *Otto.*
(Chile)

COLOUR: Dull green body, ash-grey spines with brown tips. A small amount of white wool in areoles.

SIZE: Actual size shown of plant photographed.

NOTE: Very slow growing species. Rare in collections and requiring a very open soil and much less than average water at all times.

Likes a sunny position in summer but will stand very cold in winter.

Ferocactus acanthodes *Lem.*
(California)

COLOUR: Dull green to greyish. Spines varying between bright pink and dull yellow.

SIZE: Actual size of small specimen shown.

NOTE: One of the very beautiful *Ferocacti*, its spine colours always attractive.

Rich leafmould soil but with good drainage, and slight winter warmth is to be preferred.

Slow growing, rather shallow rooted, a wide pot or pan being most suited to this species.

Ferocactus latispinus *Haw.*
(Mexico)

COLOUR: Rich green body with paler colouring on ribs. Spines red and whitish, very strong.

SIZE: Actual size of plant shown.

NOTE: An easy growing plant from seed, requiring a rich soil, plenty of water during warm weather and the usual winter rest. Specimens can become marked in winter or following spring. After a winter with high humidity, a minimum temperature of 45°F (8°C) is preferable.

Ferocactus melocactiformis *De Cand.*
(Mexico)

COLOUR: Light green plant, horny yellow spines, reddish on lower half
nearer areoles.

SIZE: Very slightly reduced.

NOTE: Not difficult to grow from seed, but young plants do better if
kept slightly warmer in winter. More mature plants stand dry cold well.

Average water, good soil drainage and winter rest.

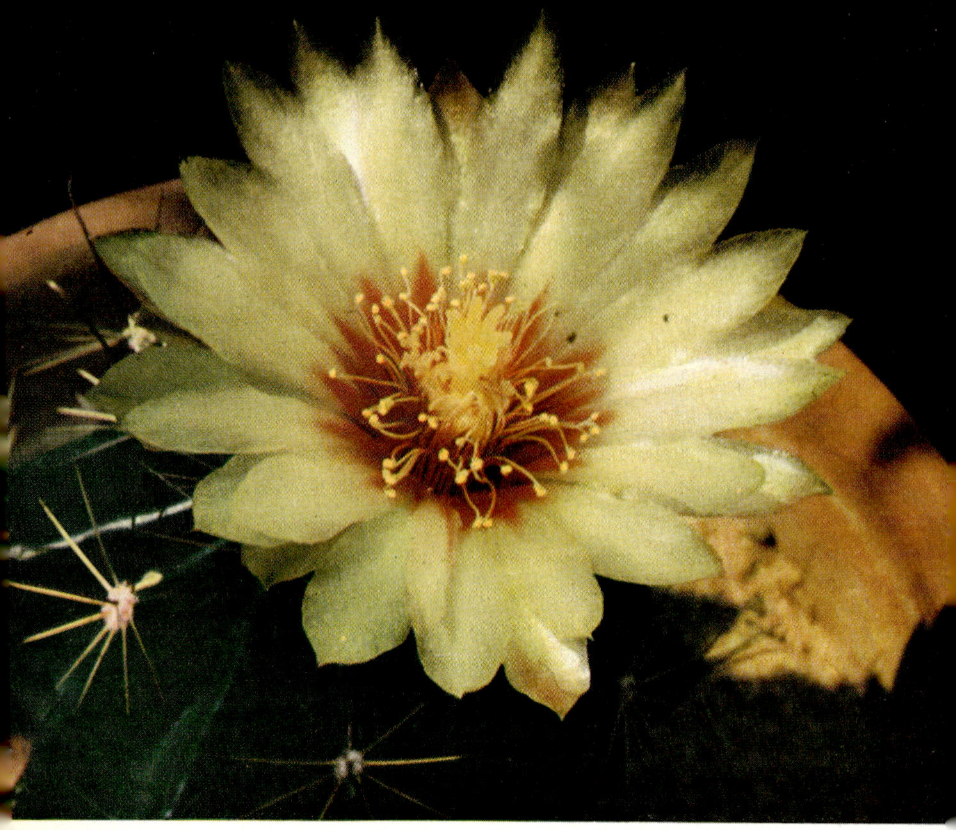

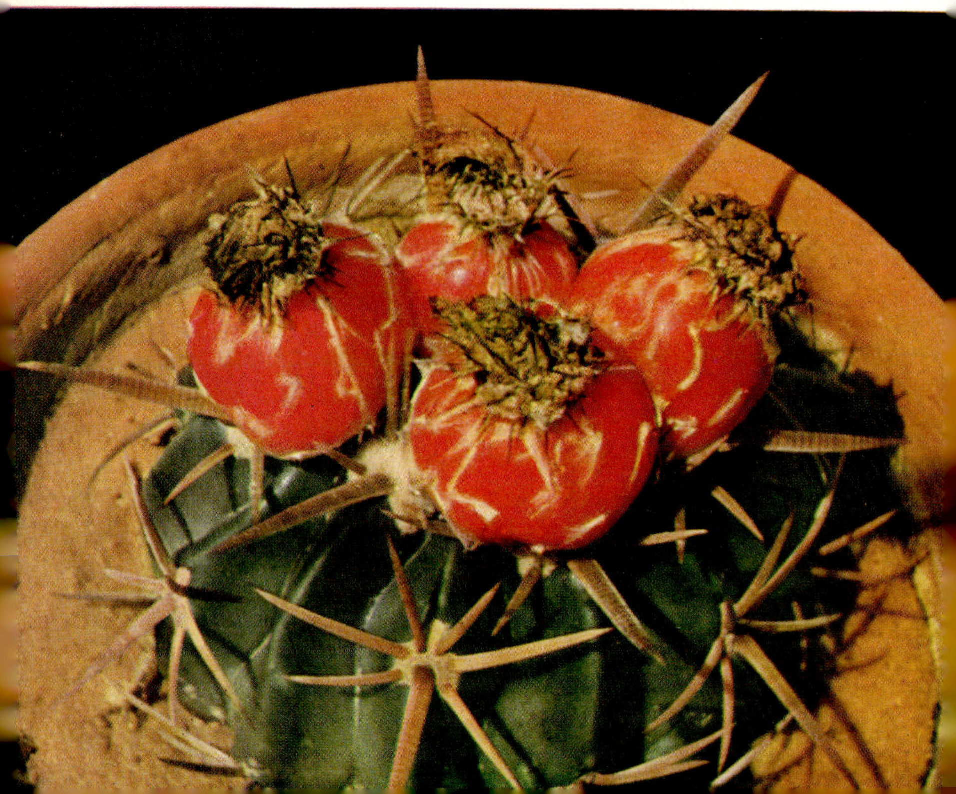

LIII   *These species belong to the* ECHINOCACTUS GROUP

Hamatocactus setispinus *B. & R.*
(Texas)

See page 391 for Notes on this species.

LIV

Homalocephala texensis *B. & R.*
(Texas)

NOTE: Requires a wide pan in which to expand, not as slow in growth as often believed. Hot conditions for flowering, a good rich leafmould soil with free drainage and dry winter resting period.

Flowers about 2 in. (5 cm) across, feather-edged and pinkish.

E*

Ferocactus wislizenii *Engelm.*

(New Mexico)

COLOUR: Usually a dark green. Spines being pink and white, the newer spines being red-brown.

SIZE: Plant photographed shown slightly reduced.

NOTE: Quite an easy plant to grow. Normal conditions of soil, water and winter rest apply to this plant.

Dry winter cold does no harm.

Gymnocalycium mihanovichii *B. & R.*
(Paraguay)

COLOUR: Plants are deep green to bronze or often quite reddish. Spines grey to yellow.

SIZE: Shown at about double actual size.

FLOWER: Green to yellow-green, slightly pink-tinged at times.

NOTE: A very easy, free-flowering little species.
Grown in a rich leafmould soil, a warm sunny greenhouse position and plenty of water in growing months, this plant will often flower over many of the summer months. Where several plants are grown together in a wide pan, flowering on one or more may be almost throughout the spring, summer and autumn, even early winter.
Can be grown indoors, but flowering not so free.

LV   *These species belong to the* ECHINOCACTUS GROUP

Gymnocalycium saglione *B. & R.*

(Argentina)

NOTE: Two forms of this fine species are shown, and others are known. The free flowering qualities of this species is quite amazing.

Likes a lot of water throughout the growing and flowering season, but should be quite dry in winter when it stands dry cold well. The plant shown on the left is in a 6-in. (15 cm) pan. These plants can attain giant dimensions for this genus.

LVI

Gymnocalycium oenanthemum *Bckbg.*

(Argentina)

NOTE: One of the most beautiful species for its flowers, requires very hot conditions for blooms to fully open.

Will stand winter cold well if dry, this being essential for flowering the following season. Growing in a 4-in. (10·2 cm) pan.

Water about average during summer months.

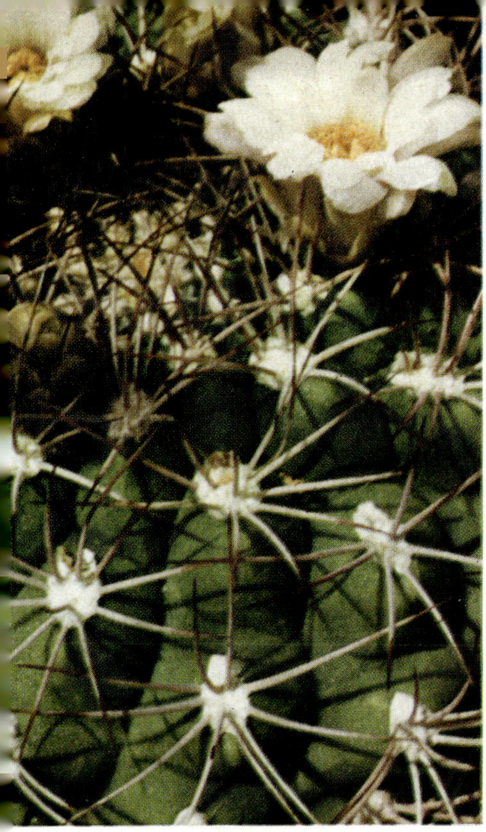
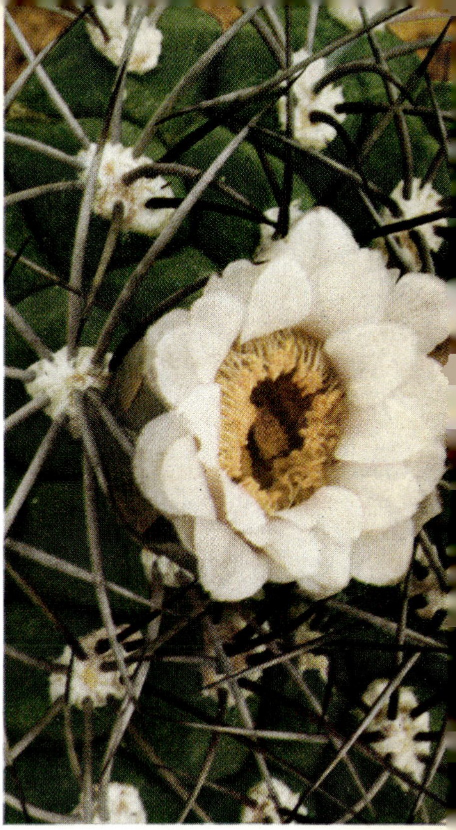
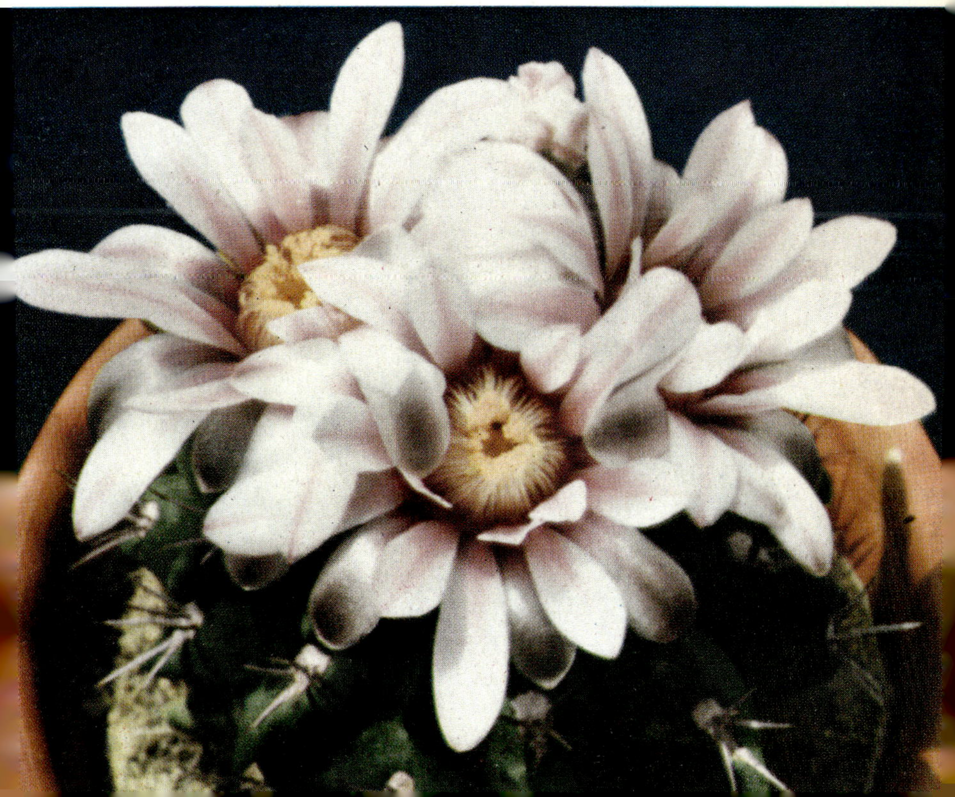

Gymnocalycium quehlianum *Berger.*
(Argentina)

COLOUR: Dull blue-green, the " chins " between areoles often bronzed Spines greyish-yellow.

SIZE: Slightly enlarged.

FLOWER: White becoming rich red in centre.

NOTE: A very easy plant to grow and flower. Likes hot sunshine for flower to open fully. Normal dry winter rest, a good soil and average water throughout summer months.

Flowers over many summer months.

Hamatocactus setispinus *B. & R.*
(S. Texas)

COLOUR: Green to reddish plants, spines varied in colour, quite often reddish, others white.

SIZE: Actual size shown above.

NOTE: A very easy, free-flowering species, the flowers being very large, often over 2 in. (5 cm) in diameter, satin yellow with red in centre.

Fruits most attractive also.

With a rich soil, plenty of water throughout growing and flowering months and kept dry in coldest winter periods, this plant will do well, often flowering at intervals over several months.

Can be grown indoors but flowers not so easy.

391

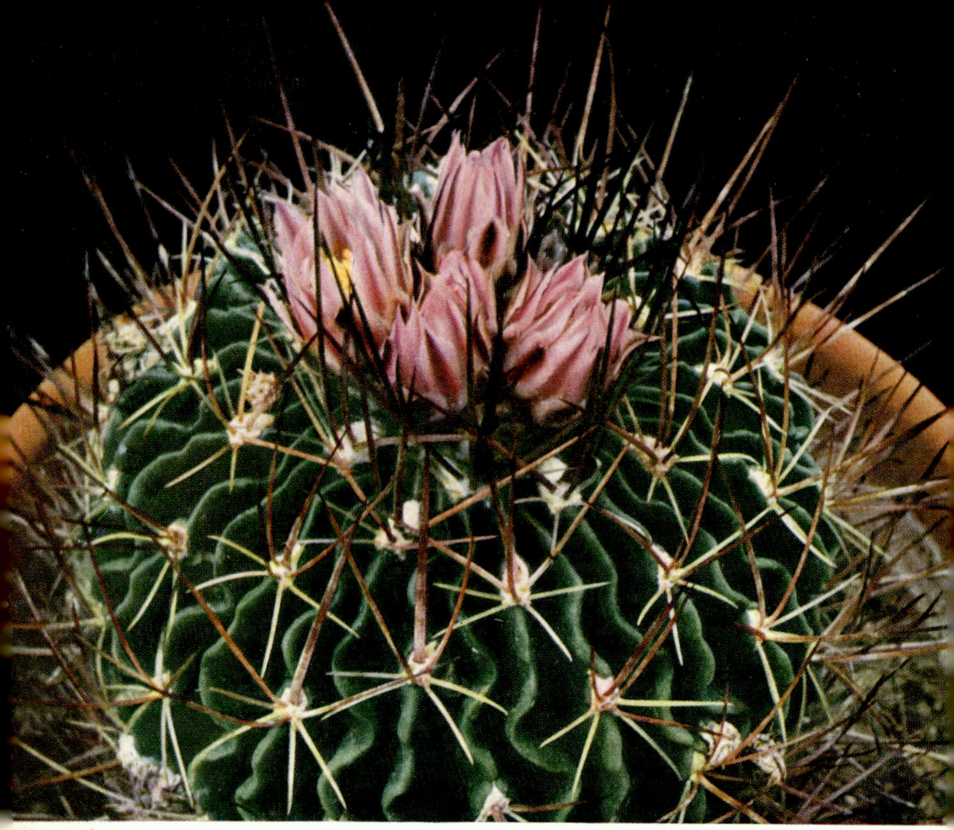
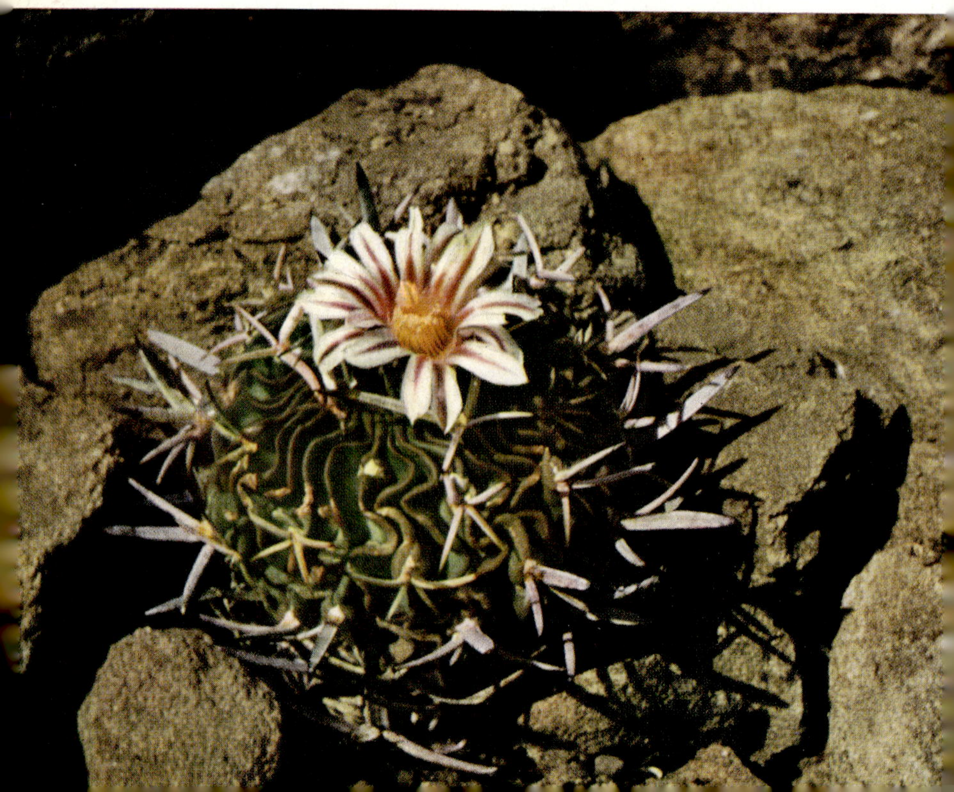

LVII   *These species belong to the* ECHINOCACTUS GROUP

Stenocactus (Echinofossulocactus) crispatus *De Cand.*
(Mexico)

NOTE: Very sandy, well-drained soil essential to this species, average or rather less water during most of the growing season.

Variable in form, this plant is always admired in any collection. If quite dry, withstands winter cold well.

The plant pictured is in a 4-in. (10·2 cm) pan.

LVIII
Stenocactus (Echinofossulocactus) pentacanthus *Berger*
(Mexico)

NOTE: A smaller growing species. flowering quite freely, each measuring about $\frac{3}{4}$ in. (1·9 cm).

Cultivation as for above.

MAMMILLARIA GROUP

Additional to Volume I, I am including here four extra genera: *Cochemiea, Epithelantha, Mamillopsis* and *Pelecyphora*.

Cochemiea is rare in collections, very slow of growth but eventually forming groups of erect or sprawling stems and with hooked spines.

Epithelantha is a true " dwarf ". It produces many flowers and fruits throughout most of each year.

Mamillopsis is not common in collections; its flowers are rather spectacular as will be seen in the colour photograph.

Pelecyphora, as can be seen in the colour photograph, is a plant of unusual form—notably the " hatchet-shaped " tubercles.

Mammillarias are known to a great many collectors, being generally regarded as all having very small flowers " ringing " the top of each plant.

While this is true of many, some lesser-known species have quite large blooms for the size of plant, often producing these singly or a few at one time.

I have included several of these among the colour photographs, to illustrate these differences. Colours such as purple, pink and bright yellow are a few of the shades which may be found on some of these lesser-known species.

Cochemiea poselgeri *B. & R.*
(Lower California)

COLOUR: Purple-bronze to green body, corky on old parts of stems. Spines off-white with red-brown tips, old spines becoming greyish.

SIZE: Shown slightly enlarged.

NOTE: Slow growing, branching near the base and becoming semi-prostrate.

Much less than average water required with very open, quick draining soil. Some winter warmth is advised but the plant requires the usual dry period of rest.

395

These species belong to the ECHINOCACTUS GROUP

Toumeya papyracantha *B. & R.*
(New Mexico)

NOTE: Rare in collections, this plant is not a large or fast grower. It requires a very well-drained and sandy soil but does particularly well with leafmould content.

Water rather less than average at all times and none in winter when it will stand dry cold without harm. Temperatures below freezing point will do no harm if quite dry.

The plant shown is in a 4-in. (10·2 cm) pot.

Toumeya schmiedickeana *Bravo and Marshall*
(Mexico)

NOTE: A slow and small growing plant, rare in collections but not difficult to keep, as the same treatment as above also suits this species.

This plant is usually the first globular cactus to flower in " The Exotic Collection " each year, usually around the end of February. Flowers are fragrant.

(Formerly known as a *Strombocactus*.)

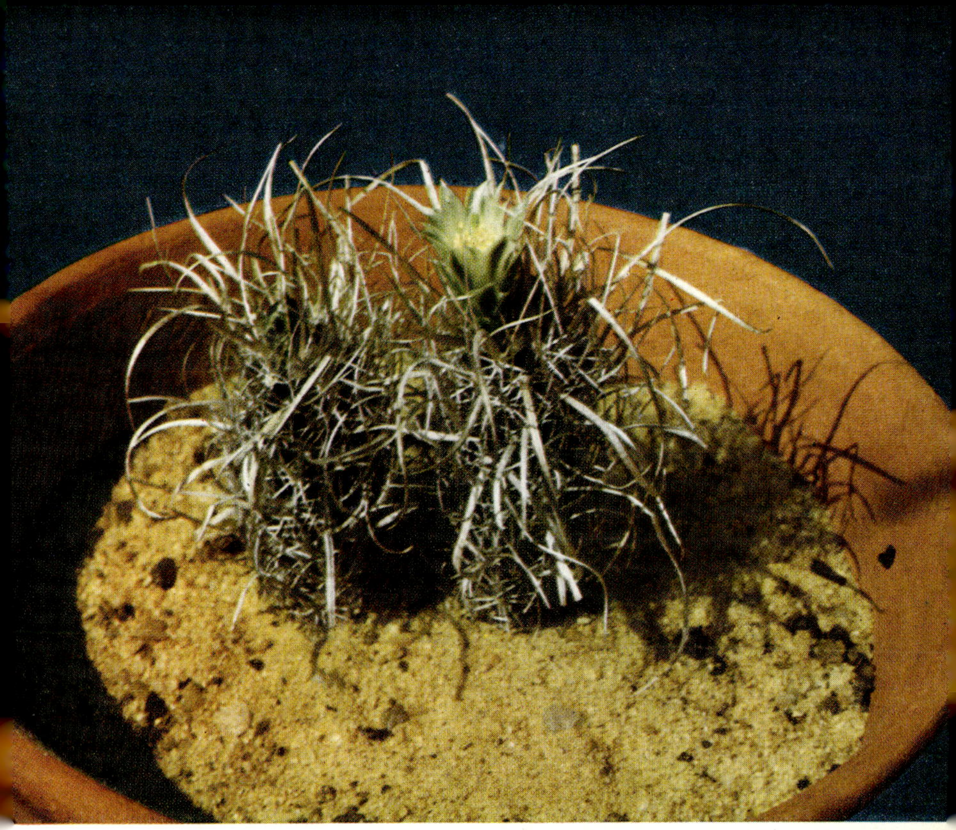

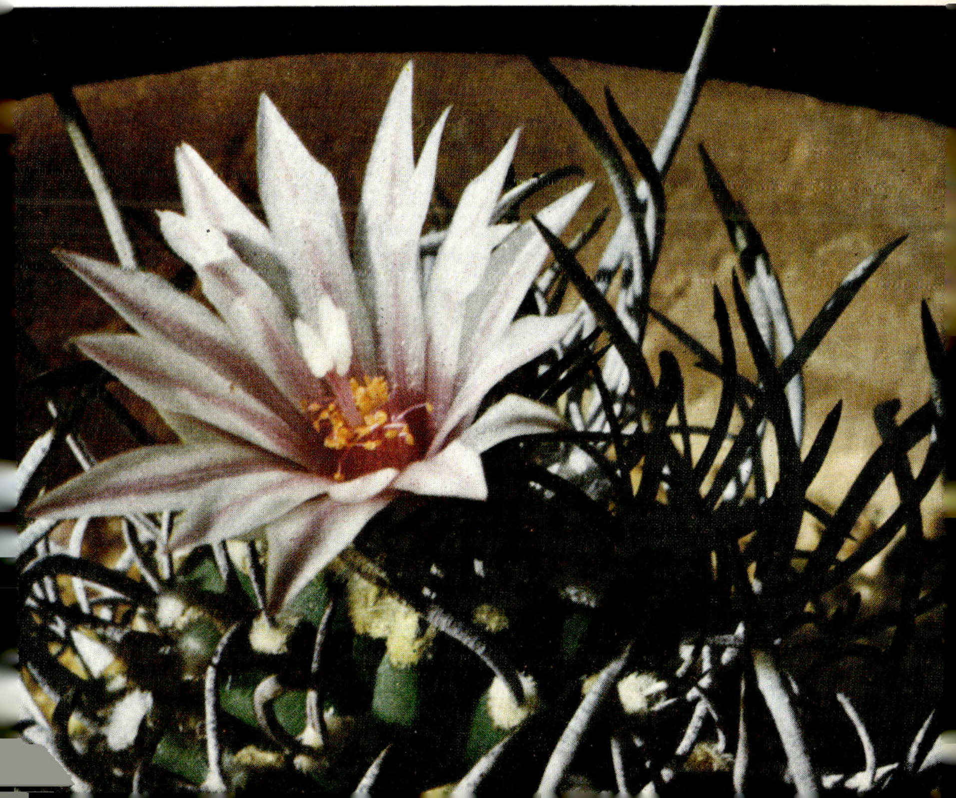

Coryphantha recurvata *B. & R.*
(Arizona)

COLOUR: Green with golden spines, those near centre of plant being brown.

SIZE: Actual size of plant photographed.

NOTE: Normal cultivation for such cacti, but with rather extra water when in actual growth.

Slow growing, eventually forming into large clusters.

Coryphantha robustispina *B. & R.*
(Arizona)

COLOUR: Rather dull green, spines pinkish-white with brown tips, old
ones being grey. White wool in centre of plant.

SIZE: Shown slightly enlarged.

NOTE: Slow growing and not difficult but likes extra watering during hot
weather, otherwise normal.

In winter, this plant tends to shrink when it will withstand quite low
temperatures, dry conditions being essential.

These species belong to the MAMMILLARIA GROUP

Coryphantha neo-mexicana *B. & R.*

(Mexico and New Mexico)

NOTE: Requires plenty of water when growing throughout the summer months and a very dry winter resting period, when it will stand cold without harm.

Slow growing, normally forming into small clusters and flowering as shown. Note the fringed petals.

Bottom
LXII

Coryphantha vivipara *B. & R.*

(N. America)

NOTE: Producing its attractive " fringed " flowers around mid-summer, this is another of the species which stands dry winter cold very well. Some forms of this species are found in Canada and these are particularly hardy. Flowers fragrant.

The plant pictured is in a 4-in. (10·2 cm) pan. Treatment as above.

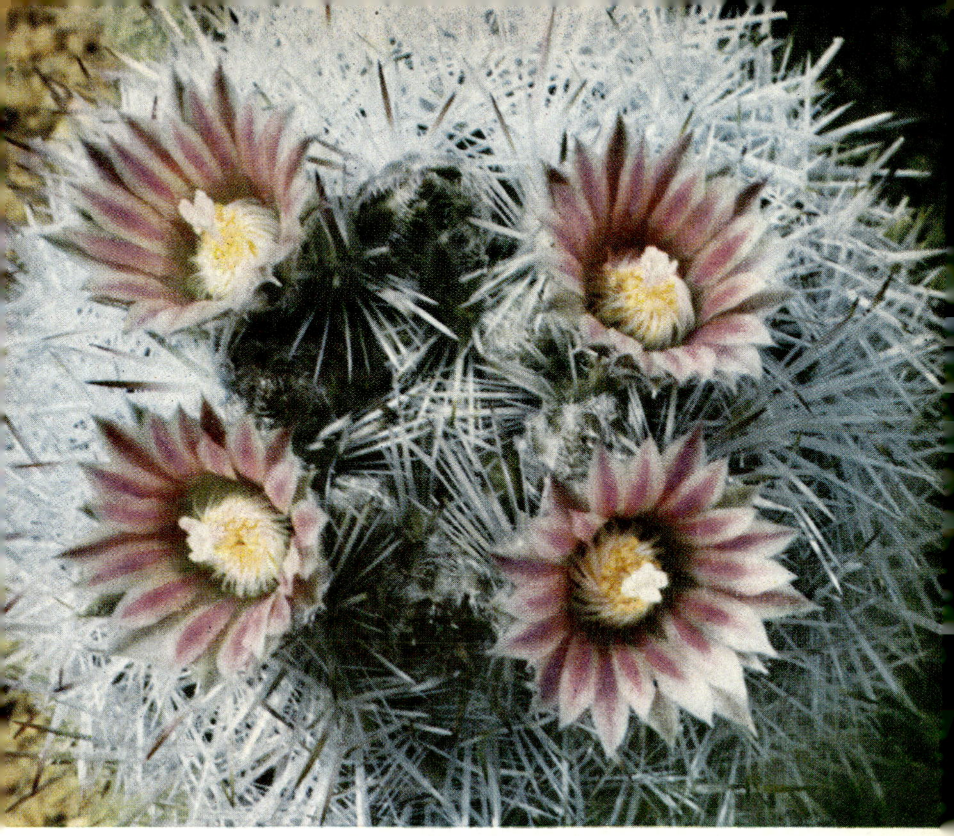
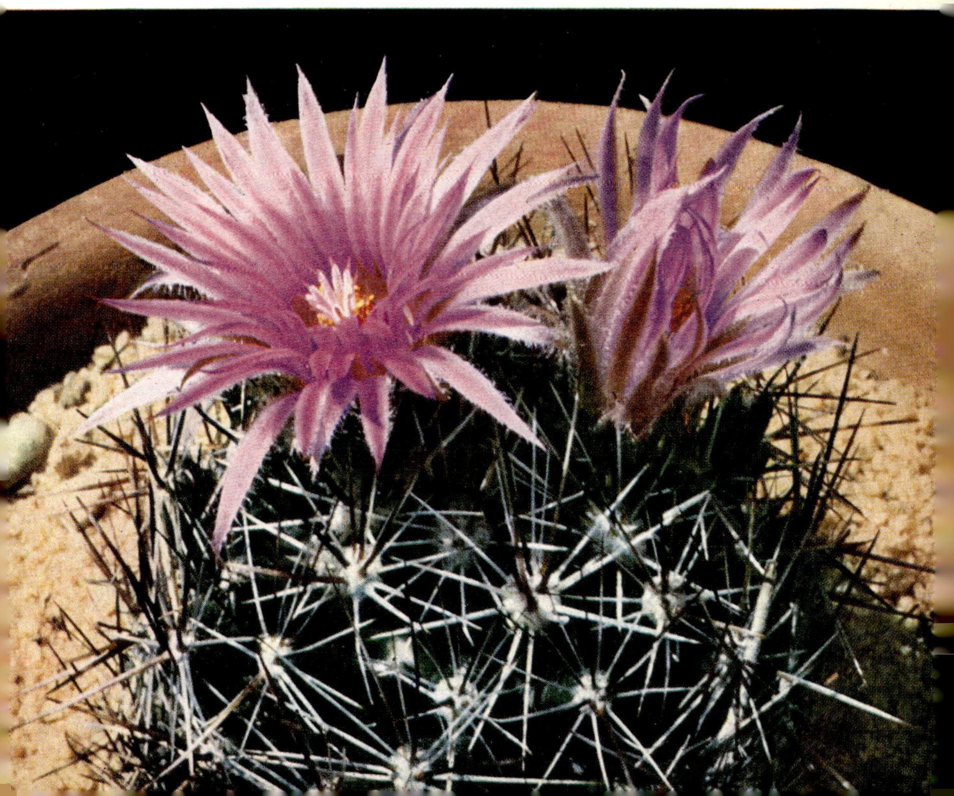

Mammillaria albescens *Tieg.*
(Mexico)

COLOUR: Pale green with white spines.

SIZE: Plant shown is growing in a 2½-in. (6.3 cm) pot.

FLOWER: White.

NOTE: A compact-growing dwarf species, likes average water when in growth or flower, a rich soil. Provided it is very dry in winter, cold will do no harm.

Mammillaria martinezii *Tieg. ex-Neale*
(Mexico)

COLOUR: Body of plant almost hidden with the many small spine-clusters. Radial spines are white and very short central (when present) is black.

SIZE: Slightly enlarged.

FLOWER: Pink with darker mid-stripe.

NOTE: Very slow growing—yet will take free watering in spring and summer when many flowers are produced as shown. Not likely to harm in very cold dry winter conditions.

This species is very solid, contrary to many speculative references which have been made from time to time by those *not* possessing the true species.

403

These species belong to the MAMMILLARIA GROUP

Coryphantha hesteri *Wright*
(Texas)

NOTE: A small growing plant, producing large flowers for its size. Average watering during growing season and dry in winter. Stands dry winter cold quite well.

Epithelantha micromeris *Weber*
(Arizona)

NOTE: Dwarf, very slow-growing and requiring extra care in drainage with a sandy soil. Water lightly at all times and keep dry in winter Flowers in spring, lasting only a few hours. Very small, pink.

Mamillopsis senilis *Weber*
(Mexico)

NOTE: One of the rarer species coming from a high altitude habitat where dry cold does the plant no harm. In cultivation, it has been found that damp cold atmospheres are to be avoided if possible, otherwise cold winter conditions are satisfactory.

Water with care at all times. The plant pictured measures about 3 in. (7·6 cm) across.

Pelecyphora aselliformis *Ehrbg.*
(Mexico)

NOTE: Growing in a 3-in. (7·6 cm) pot, this is a dwarf, slow-growing species. It requires careful watering at all times, a very open and well-drained soil, yet does well with some leafmould in the soil. Flowers open in hot sunshine.

LXVII
These species belong to the MAMMILLARIA GROUP

Mammillaria albilanata *Bckbg*.
(Mexico)

NOTE: The plant pictured is in a 2½-in. (6·3 cm) pot and can be described as a " true dwarf ". Flowers freely in early spring.

Normal watering, a rich soil and dry cold winter conditions suit it well.

LXVIII

Mammillaria gummifera *Engelm*.
(Mexico)

NOTE: Another " dwarf " shown in a 2½-in. (6·3 cm) pot, its flowers being large for the type of plant.

Treatment as above.

LXIX

Mammillaria herrerae *Werd*.
(Mexico)

NOTE: Another large-flowered species—yet " dwarf ". Requires very open sandy soil and a sunny position for best flowering.

Stands cold in winter very well in dry positions.

LXX

Mammillaria surculosa *Boed*.
(Mexico)

NOTE: Forming into clusters, this plant likes a fair amount of water when growing, a well-drained soil with some leafmould.

Growing in a 3-in. (7·6 cm) pan, it will be seen that the flowers are quite large for the type of plant.

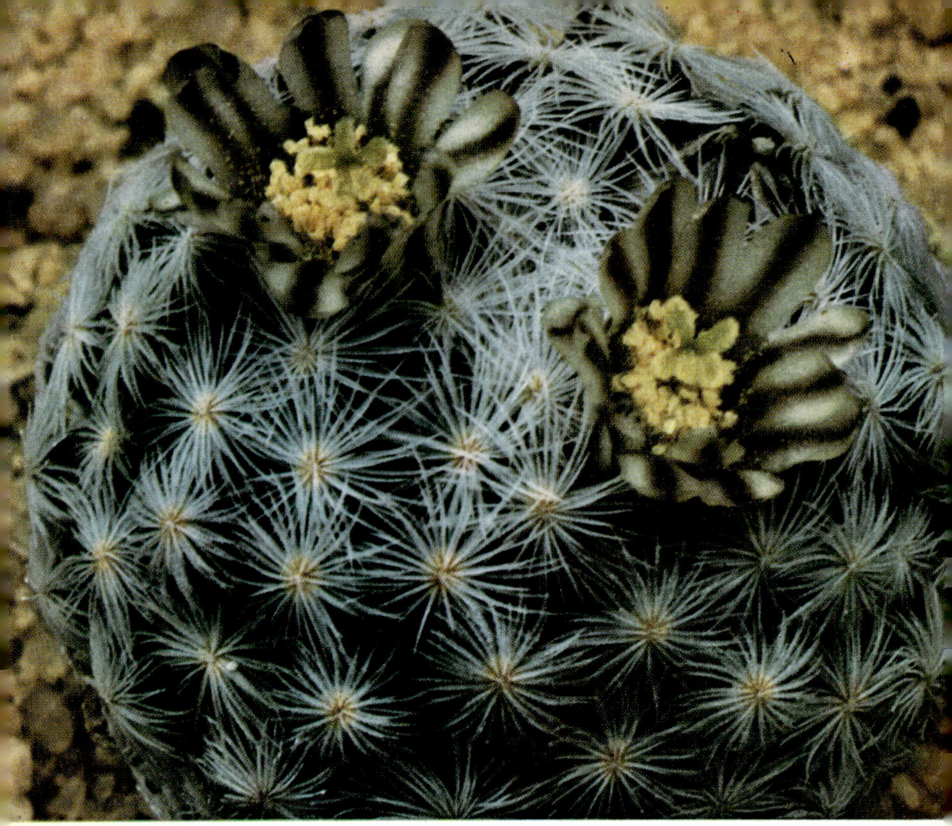

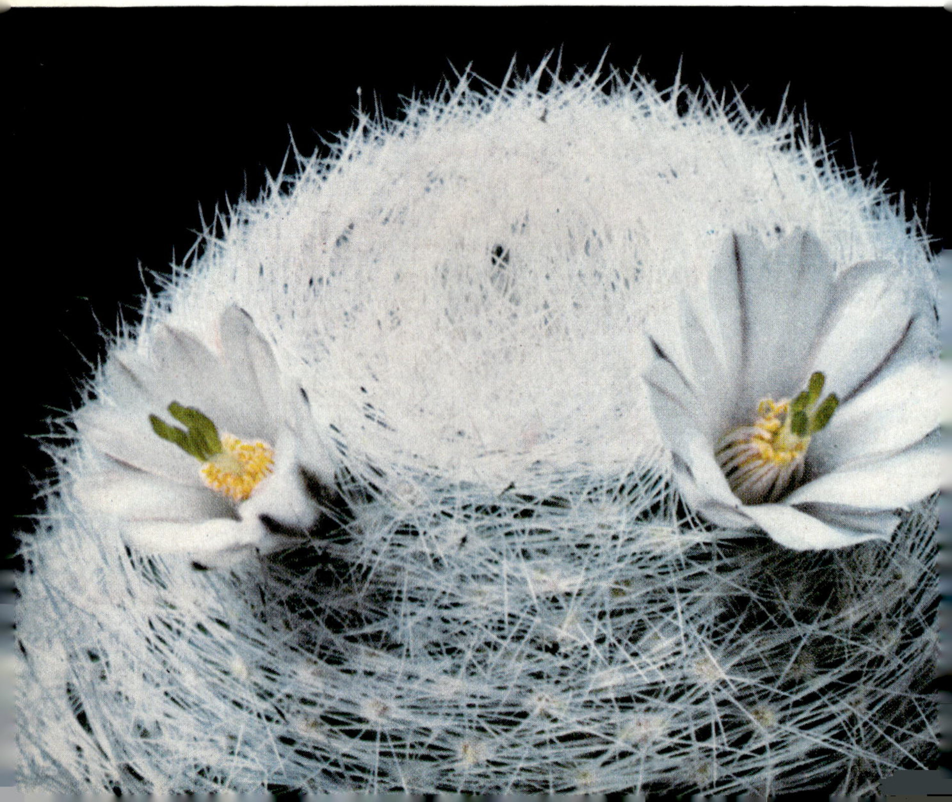

LXXI   *These species belong to the* MAMMILLARIA GROUP

Mammillaria lasiacantha *Engelm.*
(New Mexico)

NOTE: The plant pictured measures slightly over 1 in. (2·54 cm) across. A variable species in flower and spine form, some being so densely spined as to obscure completely the body colour.

Very sandy soil, a sunny position. Stands winter cold quite well when dry.

LXII

Mammillaria lenta *Brand.*
(Mexico)

NOTE: A very slow-growing species, which does not flower so easily as some. Measuring slightly over 2 in. (5 cm) in diameter, it requires less than average water at all times. An open soil is advised with a sunny position for best chance of flowering. Stands dry cold in winter without harm.

Mammillaria parkinsonii *Erbg.*
(Mexico)

COLOUR: Pale blue-green body, spines white but changing to pinkish brown near the tips.

SIZE: Plant photographed is shown slightly reduced.

FLOWER: Creamy-yellow with darker mid-stripe.

NOTE: Very slow growing, robust species. Not difficult but requiring less than average water at all times and a very long dry rest in winter when cold does no harm.

410

Mammillaria tiegeliana *Schmoll ex-Neale*
(Mexico)

COLOUR: Almost entirely pure white spines covering the plant.

SIZE: The plant photographed is shown above at approximately half its actual size.

NOTE: A very slow grower, requires open sandy soil, and much below average watering except in hot weather or when plant is in flower.

Small pink flowers may ring the heads in summer or even autumn but flowering is not so easy as with many other *Mammillarias*.

Dry in winter, these plants stand cold without harm.

411

LXXIII

These species belong to the MAMMILLARIA GROUP

Mammillaria fasciculata *Engelm.*

(Arizona)

NOTE: An attractive flowering species, rare in collections but not difficult to grow. The heads become prostrate as branches form nearer the base to cluster eventually.

With very sandy, leafmould soil and much less water than average, this plant will do well. (Now often known as *M. thornberi*.)

LXXIV

Mammillaria microcarpa *Engelm.*

(Texas)

NOTE: Growing in a 3-in. (7·6 cm) pan, this is yet another of the large-flowered species for the type of plant.

Water fairly freely when flowering and in growth, keep dry in winter.

LXXV

Mammillaria ortiz-rubiona *Werd.*

(Mexico)

NOTE: Slow-growing but forming into clusters and requiring good drainage, average water or slightly under and a dry winter position.

The plant head shown in flower measures about 3 in. (7·6 cm) in diameter.

LXXVI

Mammillaria sempervivi *Cand.*

(Mexico)

NOTE: Slow-growing but free-flowering. Shown in a 3-in. (7·6cm) pan, this plant does well with average to slightly less water and a sandy, well-drained soil but containing some leafmould.

LXXVII   *These species belong to the* EPIPHYLLUM AND PHYLLOCACTUS GROUP

Phyllocactus hybrid *Hort.*

NOTE: A very rich leafmould soil, some manure being used where possible. Grow in slight shade, warm and humid with some water and warmth in winter.

Note the almost fluorescent petals. About 7 in. (17·8 cm) across.

LXXVIII

Phyllocactus hybrid *Hort.*

NOTE: Treatment as above. This hybrid is of rather different flower-form, being between *Hylocereus* and *Phyllocactus*.

Measuring over 7 in. (17·8 cm) in diameter—fragrant, remaining open 2–3 days.

LXXIX

Rhipsalidopsis rosea *B. & R.*
(S. Brazil)

NOTE: One of the most beautiful, dwarf-growing epiphytes. Each flower measures almost 1 in. (2·54 cm).

Does not require grafting for easy flowering. If grown in a soil containing 75 per cent leafmould and 25 per cent sand, a warm but humid atmosphere with " broken sunlight ", it will produce an abundance of blooms. Some water and warmth in winter.

LXXX

Schlumbergera gaertneri var. mackoyana
(Brazil)

See page 418 for Notes on this species.

Mammillaria viereckii fa. cristata *Hort.*
(Mexico)

COLOUR: Rich green body almost obscured by the bright golden-
brown spines.

SIZE: Shown enlarged almost double size.

NOTE: A very rich leafmould soil, hot sunny conditions and average
water gives best results—keep quite dry in winter.

A popular plant, often grown indoors but becomes rather less compact.

Can be grown into very beautiful large specimens.

416

EPIPHYLLUM AND PHYLLOCACTUS GROUP

Epiphytic cacti have a strong appeal to many a collector, due to the beautiful flowers produced in so many colours and sizes and their ease of cultivation where some warmth in winter is convenient. The room can quite well house a few of these plants, where they often do exceptionally well.

Schlumbergera is very much like the well-known " Christmas-Cactus " in plant form, but flowering occurs at different periods of the year.

Also to be found in this group are the many horticultural hybrids of *Phyllocacti* which often produce some quite startling flowers in both colour and size. Two such blooms are shown in the colour photography, along with the quite vivid colouring of *Schlumbergera mackoyana*.

HALF-TONE PLATES
Illustrated in Volume I

Schlumbergera gaertneri var. mackoyana
(Brazil)

syn. *Rhipsalidopsis gaertneri* Moran

COLOUR: Usually a dull green leaf.

SIZE: Shown at about twice actual size.

FLOWER: See colour illustration on page 414.

NOTE: This fine epiphyte, flowering in early spring, likes a reasonably warm and humid atmosphere at all times of the year and not in full summer sun.

In habit it resembles the well-known " Christmas-cactus ". Soil should be 80 per cent pure leafmould, remainder sand.

HATIORA AND RHIPSALIS GROUP

Rhipsalidopsis rosea which is shown among the colour photographs introduces another genus not represented among the epiphytic cacti illustrated in Volume I.

It is a truly spectacular plant capable of producing some hundred or so blooms on quite a modest-sized plant.

The three *Rhipsalis* illustrated as half-tone photographs depict three different forms in this genus, including one of the larger-flowered species. The very dwarf *R. cereuscula* seen growing in a cleft on tree-bark, is one of the species which may at times produce a very long, straight, slender growth from the tip of which a new plant similar to that illustrated may form.

Rhipsalis cereuscula *Haw.*

(E. Brazil and Uruguay)

COLOUR: Bright yellow-green with whitish soft, hair-like spines.

SIZE Very slightly enlarged above natural.

NOTE: This miniature epiphyte, of very easy culture, requires a soil consisting of about 80 per cent leafmould, remainder sand.

Some warmth in winter when a little water should be given. During summer months give water very freely. Shade is important and humid conditions an advantage when its white flowers will be borne on the tips of growths.

Rhipsalis crispata *Pfeiff.*
(Brazil)

COLOUR: Pale green, paler on new branches.

SIZE: Slightly enlarged.

NOTE: One of the smaller growing epiphytes, noted for its very wavy edges.

The photograph shows one branch growing erect. Others may be produced to hang down.

Some warmth in winter is essential, a good rich leafmould soil and some water at all times of the year. Not a fast growing species.

421

Rhipsalis grandiflora *Haw.*
(E. Brazil)

COLOUR: Usually a yellow-green, the older stems develop some white spines, appressed against the stems.

SIZE: Shown at twice natural size.

FLOWER: Translucent lemon-yellow.

NOTE: Shady humid conditions with some warmth in winter is essential. Water at all times of the year as required. Grow in 80 per cent leafmould with remainder sand to conduct moisture.

Flowers usually in early spring, very profuse from almost any positions along the stems.

Part Two

SUCCULENTS
OTHER THAN CACTI

Echinocactus grusonii, Cleistocacti and *Euphorbias,* growing in part of
" The Exotic Collection ".

AGAVE

This genus was not included in the illustrations in Volume I. I am therefore including seven half-tone photographs of mostly smaller-growing species which can be accommodated by the average collector.

It is probably true to say that the majority of *Agaves* can be regarded as half-hardy in temperate climates—most will stand a few degrees of frost, perhaps even snow and frost, but they may not all stand freezing in their centres.

Agave attenuata, for example, is one which does not like cold and should be kept in the greenhouse at all times of the year due to the soft nature of its leaves. The other six species illustrated can be most advantageously grown outside in their pots for the whole of the summer and well into autumn, being taken into the greenhouse for the worst winter months. *Agave lophantha*, however, is more hardy than the others and I have wintered it out-of-doors in a well-drained rockery without any protection when the temperature fell to 0° F. (— 18°C.)

Some species produce branches from underground, even at a distance from the parent plant, while others do not branch at all or very rarely so and have to be reproduced from seed.

Some of the half-hardy *Agaves* can be grown and wintered in a well-drained rockery if some protection is given to prevent the centres from wet. It is this wet becoming frozen which can damage or kill a plant—dry cold with quite low temperatures rarely causes harm.

Agave americana *Trel.* var. mediopicta
fa. alba. *Hort.*
(Horticultural Origin)

COLOUR: Dark blue-green leaves with off-white mid-stripe. Thorns on leaf edges and tip are brown.

SIZE: Shown at about $\frac{1}{4}$ actual size of plant photographed.

NOTE: This rare *Agave* does produce a few branches from underground even when quite small.

Likes a lot of water, plenty of root space in which to develop and branch, stands dry winter cold well.

Agave attenuata *Salm.*
(Mexico)

COLOUR: Very pale green, soft succulent leaves, *not* armed with a sharp point at the leaf tips as in most *Agaves*.

SIZE: Plant photographed is 18 in. (45·7cm) tall. Growing in 12-in. (30.5 cm) pot.

NOTE: Fairly slow growing, eventually on a tall trunk. Likes a rich soil and plenty of water during growing season. Tender to frosts, thus requiring some winter protection, but not below 45° F (8° C).

Agave bracteosa *S. Wats.*
(Mexico)

COLOUR: Pale green leaves with a roughened surface and edge.

SIZE: Shown in a 9-in. (22·9 cm) pot.

NOTE: Very slow growing but rare *Agave* of dwarf habit. Less than average water at all times and a little warmth in winter, when it should be kept dry. Otherwise, not difficult.

Agave filifera *Salm.*
(Mexico)

COLOUR: Very dark green with white markings and hairs. Tip of leaf
is greyish.

SIZE: Specimen photographed is in a 9-in. (22·9 cm) pot.

NOTE: Slow growing, remaining low to the ground but producing some
branches.

A rich soil and plenty of water suits this species well. Stands dry, very cold
winter conditions.

Agave lophantha *Schied.*
(Mexico)

COLOUR: Dark blue-green with lighter mid-stripe, margins and tips
being ash-grey.

SIZE: Growing in a 9-in. (22·9 cm) pot.

NOTE: A variable species of which a number of forms are known,
capable of withstanding many degrees of frost in the open.
Slow growing, water about average but likes a very well drained soil.

Agave parviflora *Torr.*
(Mexico and Arizona)

COLOUR: Dull green leaves with white markings and hairs, a brown thorn on the tip of each leaf.

SIZE: Actual size shown.

NOTE: This is a young specimen shown above, large plants being perhaps 6 in. (15 cm) in diameter.

Easy to grow, a rich soil, plenty of water during the warmer months suits this species, in winter, cold dry treatment is ideal.

Agave toumeyana *Trel.*
(Arizona)

COLOUR: Bright but dark green leaves with fibrous white hairs. Also streaked with white and having sharp brown thorns.

SIZE: Growing in a 9-in. (22·8 cm) pot.

NOTE: Slow growing but makes a lot of root, hence the rather large pot is to be preferred.
Stands winter cold well if dry, otherwise very easy of culture.

431

LXXXI   *These species belong to the* ALOE GROUP

Aloe saponaria *Haw.*
(Cape Province)

See page 443 for Notes on this species.

LXXXII

Aloe arborescens *Mill.*
(Cape Province)

NOTE: A useful plant for winter flowering and indoor decoration. Buds begin to form during late autumn and the flowers around January and February.

With a rich leafmould soil, plenty of water and extra autumn warmth, flowering may be brought forward to December; otherwise the plants stand cold indoor conditions very well.

Flower spikes extend about 18 in. (45·7 cm) above the plant.

ALOE

Aloes generally attract many a collector but in countries where greenhouses are essential, these plants are often only sparsely represented, due to the amount of room required to house them in winter.

There are, however, quite a number of either dwarf or " nonspreading " species which might well be included among collections. Many will produce tall flower-spikes at various times of the year and allowed to are well worth growing.

Aloe arborescens, for example, if allowed to grow wild, will form into a much-branched bush, but a single stem can be grown and flowered in a 9-in. (22·9 cm) pot. The small branches need not be allowed to develop if room is limited.

The slow-growing " Tree-Aloes "—*A. dichotoma, A. pillansii* and *A. ramosissima*—are far from common in collections, yet when grown from seed make interesting specimens as they do not take up much room.

Two differing forms of flower-spikes are shown in colour: *A. arborescens* (usually about January) and *A. saponaria*, which during the summer months has a " branched " inflorescence.

HALF-TONE PLATES
Illustrated in Volume I

Aloe brevifolia *Mill.*
(Cape Province)

COLOUR: Light green leaves, edged greenish-white.

SIZE: Natural size shown.

NOTE: A low-growing species which branches freely, does not develop a wide leaf spread and is very suited to the small greenhouse.

Free-flowering, usually in midsummer, the flower spikes attaining perhaps 18 in. in height. Flowers orange-red.

Do not over-water this species, otherwise it is not difficult of culture.

Aloe deserti *Bgr.*
(E. Africa)

COLOUR: Bright shiny green leaves with orange coloured markings.

SIZE: Actual size of plant photographed.

NOTE: Very attractively marked *Aloe*, ideal for the small greenhouse as it is not a fast grower. Eventually forms into spiral form.

Likes a rich soil, free watering in summer and some winter warmth essential, when it should be kept quite dry.

Aloe dichotoma *Masson.*
(Cape Province)

COLOUR: Pale chalky-green with creamy raised teeth.

SIZE: Actual size shown, of young plant.

NOTE: Slow growing, rather rare in collections, eventually forming a trunk which divides freely as the plant grows taller.

In growing habit, similar to *A. ramosissima.*

Slight warmth in winter advised.

Aloe eru *Bgr.*
(Eritrea)

COLOUR: Dull green leaves with cream markings and orange red edges.

SIZE: Actual size shown of plant pictured.

NOTE: Not a fast grower but quite easy of culture. Plenty of water in warmest weather, but quite dry in winter with slight warmth advised.

Good species for small collections as it does not take up too much room.

Aloe greatheadii *Schonl.*
(Bechuanaland)

COLOUR: Shiny dark green, markings white or creamy.

SIZE: Growing in 4½-in. (11·4 cm) pot.

NOTE: Requires plenty of water and a rich soil; quite an easy plant to grow, attractively marked.

Dry in winter, it stands cold quite well.

Aloe pillansii *L. Gunthrie*
(Little Namaqualand)

COLOUR: Chalky blue-green, with white teeth.

SIZE: Shown at half natural size.

NOTE: A rare *Aloe* in collections, of tree-forming type, often in habitat producing very few branches even when tall and old.

Some warmth in winter essential, average water in summer.

Aloe plicatilis *Mill.*
(Cape Province)

COLOUR: Pale green with creamy white margins.

SIZE: The leaf spread of this plant is about 2 ft. (61 cm).

NOTE: An attractive species, slow growing and of very distinctive habit, as will be noted from the photograph.

Likes plenty of water in summer months, but must be given some warmth in winter when it should be kept dry.

Aloe ramosissima *Pillans.*

(N. Namaqualand)

COLOUR: Smooth grey stems and pale or slightly chalky green leaves, yellow on edges.

SIZE: Growing in a 12-in. (30·5 cm) pot.

NOTE: Rare and slow-growing, the above plant being many years old. Its growing habit is much like the " Dragon-tree " famous on the Canary Islands (*Dracaena draco*), in miniature.

Requires slight winter warmth, good soil drainage and less than average water.

Aloe saponaria *Haw.*
(Cape Province)

COLOUR: Varying between green and pink leaves with attractive mottling.

SIZE: The plant shown measures almost 2 ft. (61 cm) across, a mature specimen.

FLOWER: See colour picture, page 433.

NOTE: Very large head of leaves can be grown on old plants with a rich soil, plenty of root room and water.

When in pots, plants tend to produce smaller heads but much more beautiful colourings.

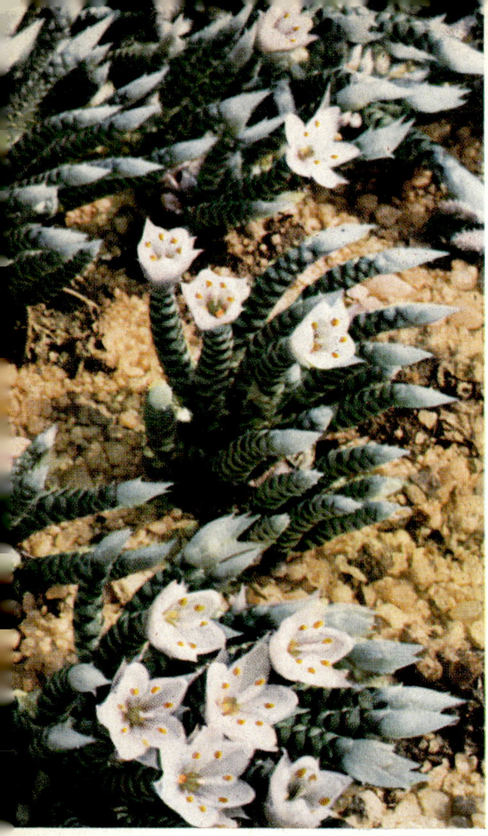

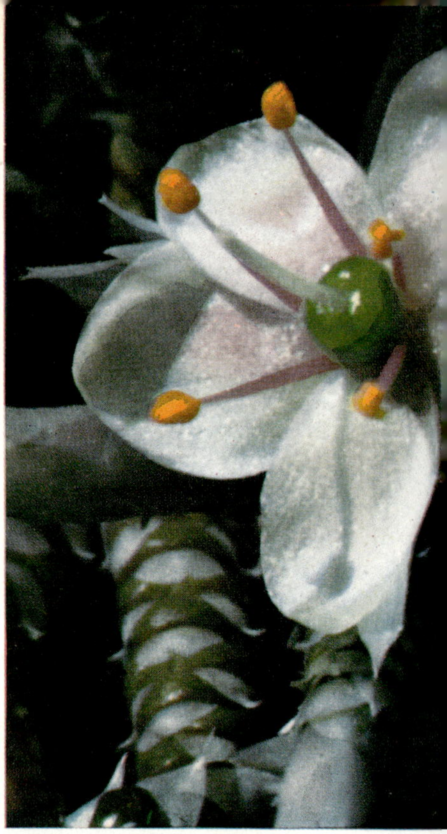

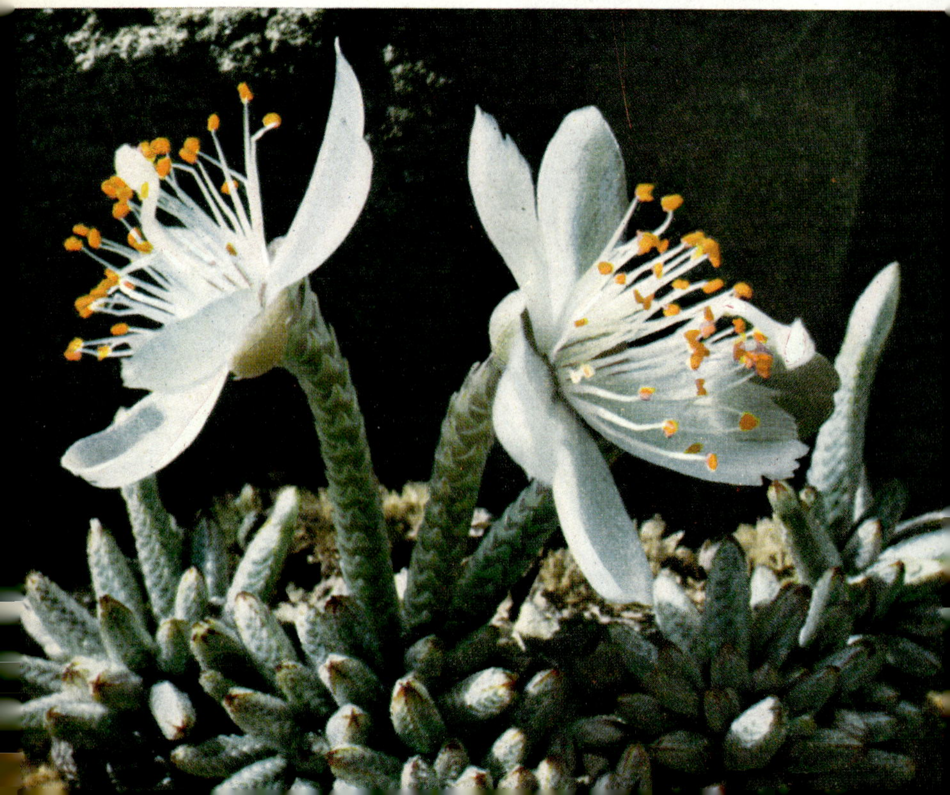

LXXXIII

Anacampseros rhodesica *N.E. Br.*

(S. Rhodesia)

These species belong to the ANACAMPSEROS GROUP

NOTE: A very beautiful and free-flowering dwarf succulent, the flowering period extending over many summer months.

A soil consisting of equal parts of leafmould and sand only suits this species extremely well. Water fairly freely during all warm months. Flowers measure slightly over $\frac{1}{4}$ in. (0·6 cm) when open during late afternoon in hot sunny weather. Slight winter warmth is essential.

Flowers are produced in succession from each of the " tails ".

LXXXIV

Anacampseros alstonii *Schonl.*

(S. and S.W. Africa)

NOTE: This species produces rather larger flowers, each measuring just over $\frac{1}{2}$ in. (1·3 cm) when fully open, but only one flower may be expected from each " tail ".

Each " tail ", when about to flower, becomes elongated as shown in the illustration.

Cultivation as for above.

ANACAMPSEROS

This genus is ideally suited to the collector with the small green-house, all plants being dwarf in nature, some very dwarf indeed.

I illustrate two species in colour and two in half-tone, three of which—*A. alstonii, A. comptonii* and *A. rhodesica*—possess large swollen roots which often appear partly above ground.

Grown from seeds, these are not difficult and will in time develop the swollen root as the number of tails or heads increase. A young plant is also able to flower although the number of blooms will, of course, be fewer.

Contrary to the belief of many, these plants are *not* difficult, provided they are given an ample supply of water *and* are grown in a sandy leafmould mixture. The reason why these fascinating little plants have been regarded as difficult has been due to their being given too little water.

HALF-TONE PLATES
Illustrated in Volume I

Anacampseros baeseckii   *Dtr.*
(Namaqualand)

COLOUR: Almost entirely covered with matted white hair.

SIZE: Shown enlarged approximately four times the plant photographed.

NOTE: Not common in collections, this species is known in many forms,
some free-branching.

Average water in summer, and a soil of equal parts of leafmould and sand
only suit this genus well.

Slight warmth in winter necessary.

447

Anacampseros comptonii *Pillans.*

(Cape Province)

COLOUR: Deep olive-green leaves, often very bronzed with a little white hair between.

SIZE: Shown at three times actual size.

FLOWER: Purple. (Flower stalks nearly same colour.)

NOTE: This little dwarf species is not common in collections today; very free flowering and of easy culture in a soil of equal parts of leafmould and sand.

Water rather less than average and very little in winter, slight warmth advised.

BOWIEA

An attractive monotypic genus, resting during the summer months and producing its delicate twining foliage and flowers in autumn and winter.

The succulent, papery-covered bulb requires to rest " on the soil " as can be seen in the photograph, and while this resting period lasts, it should not be allowed to remain absolutely without water for too long, as with many other of the deciduous succulents.

Growing from seed is quite easy, and when only six months old the bulb may well have reached the size of a " pea " or even a little larger. In this stage of the young growth, it should *not* have a resting period but be kept growing for approximately the first two years of its life.

LXXXV   *This species belongs to the* CEROPEGIA GROUP

Ceropegia bulbosa *Roxb.*
(S. Africa)

NOTE: Requires a very rich leafmould soil, a fairly large pot, in order to keep the roots cool, broken sunlight and plenty of water during all growing months. A little water also in winter when a little warmth to auoid frosts is essential.

One of the well-known " trailing " type *Ceropegias* producing many flowers during the season.

Bottom
LXXXVI   *This species belongs to the* EUPHORBIA GROUP

Euphorbia stellata *Willd.*
(Cape Province)

See page 491 for Notes on this species.

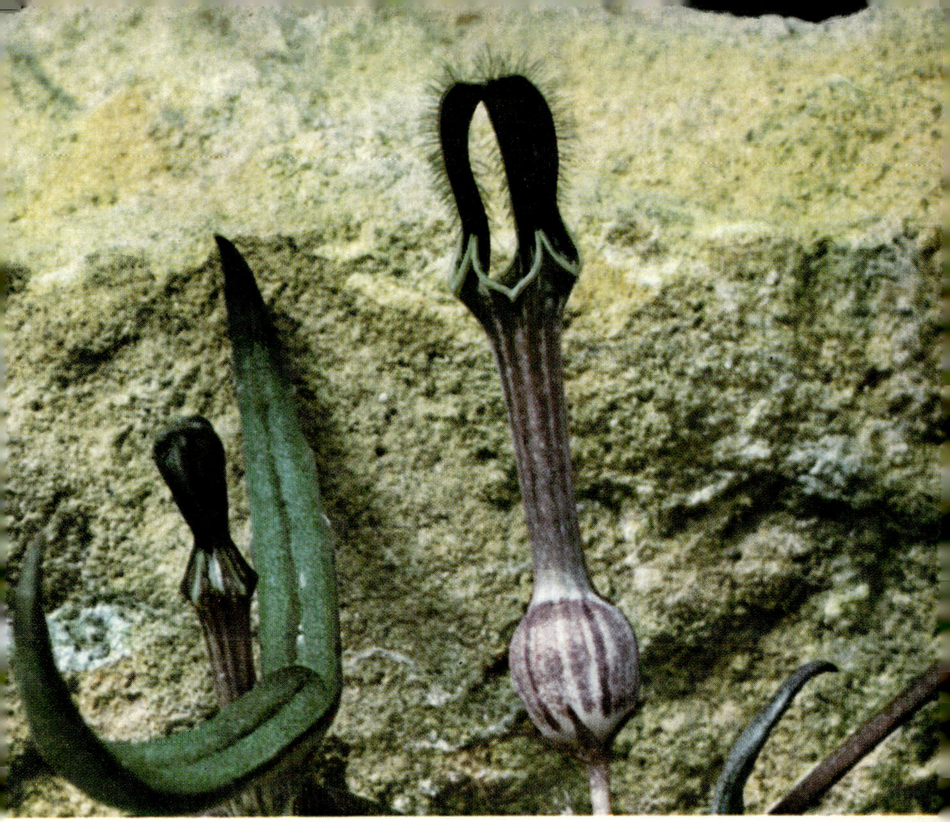

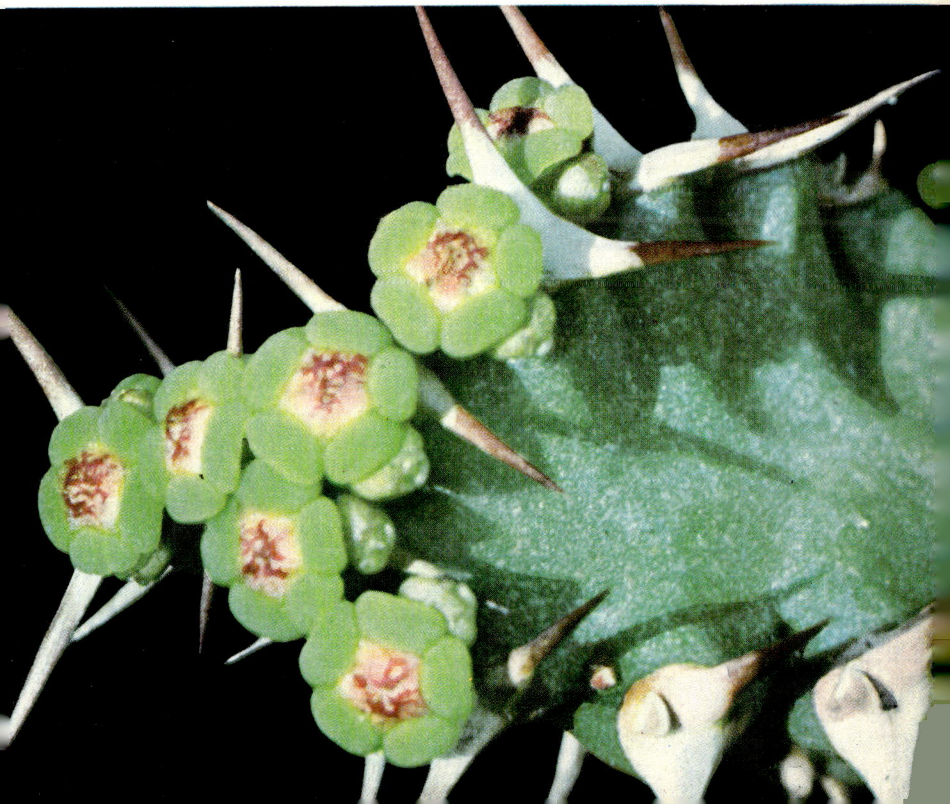

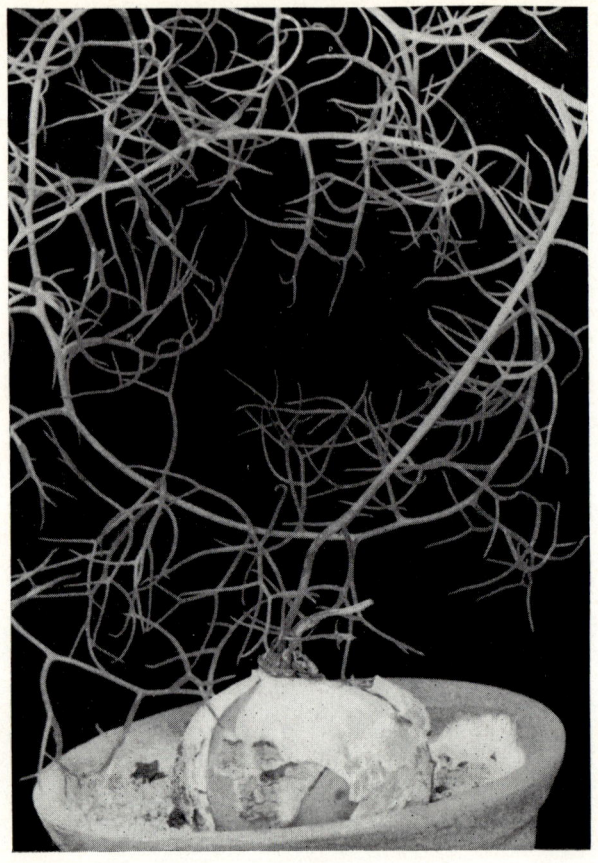

Bowiea volubilis *Harv.*
(S. Africa)

COLOUR: Pale green bulb with whitish papery surface and bright green foliage.

SIZE: Shown slightly reduced.

NOTE: Usually growing in autumn and onwards, when it produces many twining branches upon which the small green flowers appear.

Resting period usually spring and summer when all branches will have withered, leaving only the bulb. Give slight spraying in resting period, more water when growing, and keep away from frosts, some winter warmth being essential. Not difficult.

CEROPEGIA

This interesting genus is becoming very popular, the odd " lantern-like " flowers being so easily produced in great numbers along the twining stems, from the base of every leaf position.

These twining growths develop from a large swollen root in contrast to those illustrated in Volume I. This type of *Ceropegia* requires a greater amount of water and to be grown in a much larger pot than might be thought necessary for the size of plant.

Ideal for hanging down from the front of greenhouse staging or for training along any suitable position.

HALF-TONE PLATES
Illustrated in Volume I

CISSUS

This genus contains two completely contrasting forms: the thinner clambering type has its small leaves and tendrils with which in nature it climbs the trees of tropical Africa; the other type coming from the drier regions of S.W. Africa is noted for its wide-based, trunk-like stems, often reaching sizeable proportions when very old.

The latter type is grouped among the deciduous succulents, except that its leafy growing period falls within our normal summer growing season.

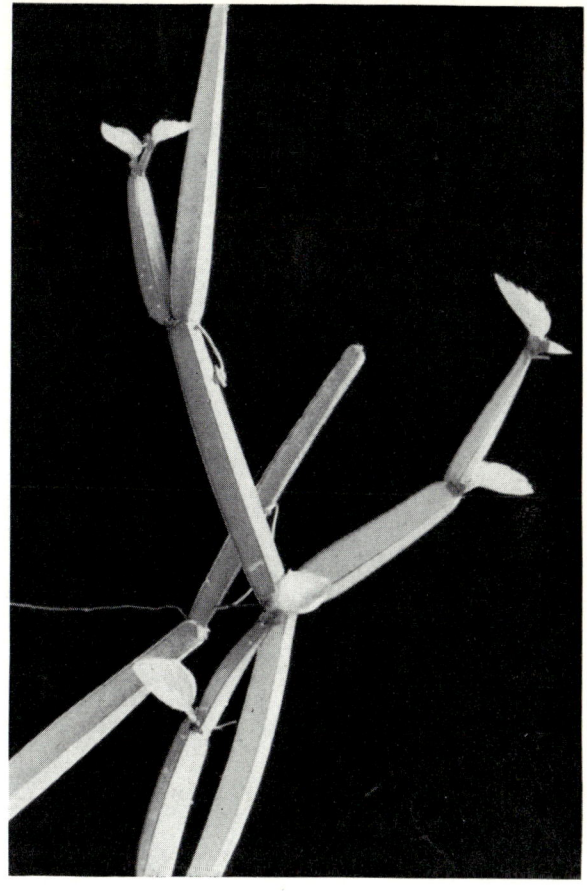

Cissus cactiformis   *Gillg.*
(S. and Tropical Africa)

COLOUR: Light green stems, edged with brown. Leaves, when present light green also.

SIZE: Part of plant shown slightly reduced.

NOTE: Likes plenty of water when growing in summer, some water in winter but must be kept in a slightly warmed temperature.

Rich soil with extra leafmould for this fast-growing and climbing succulent.

Cissus juttae   *Dtr. & Gillg.*
(S.W. Africa)

COLOUR: Greyish-brown stem with papery surface. Leaves light green often edged and veined with red.

SIZE: Shown slightly reduced.

NOTE: A deciduous succulent, but its growing period is more convenient, being in summer when it can be watered quite heavily. When resting in winter, give slight water and keep clear of frosts, a little warmth being preferable. Leaves are dropped during the resting period. (Now often known as *Cyphostemma juttae*.)

COTYLEDON

Two of the deciduous type, noted for their weird stem form, particularly in summer when without leaf, are illustrated.

These succulents are of quite easy culture, although slow of growth, provided they are allowed their normal rest which occurs during our summer. It should be mentioned that extra water in the late summer will not cause the plant to advance its growing period until it is quite ready to do so. Thus it is better to await sign of new leaves, even if quite late in the year, before increasing the amount of water as required during growth.

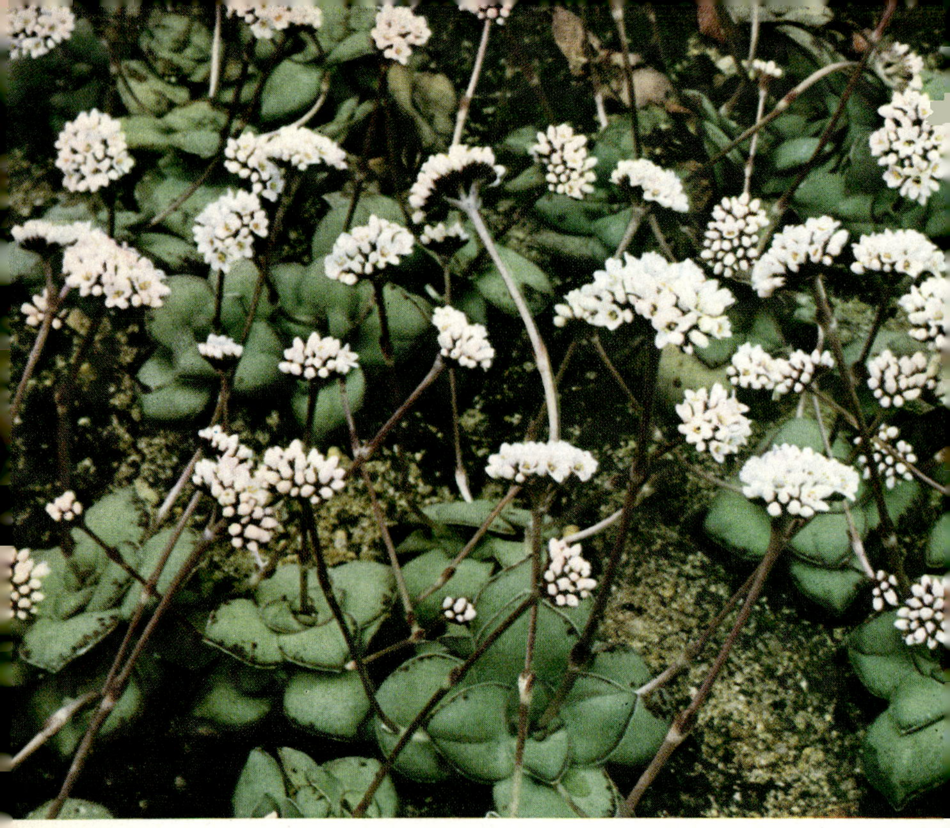

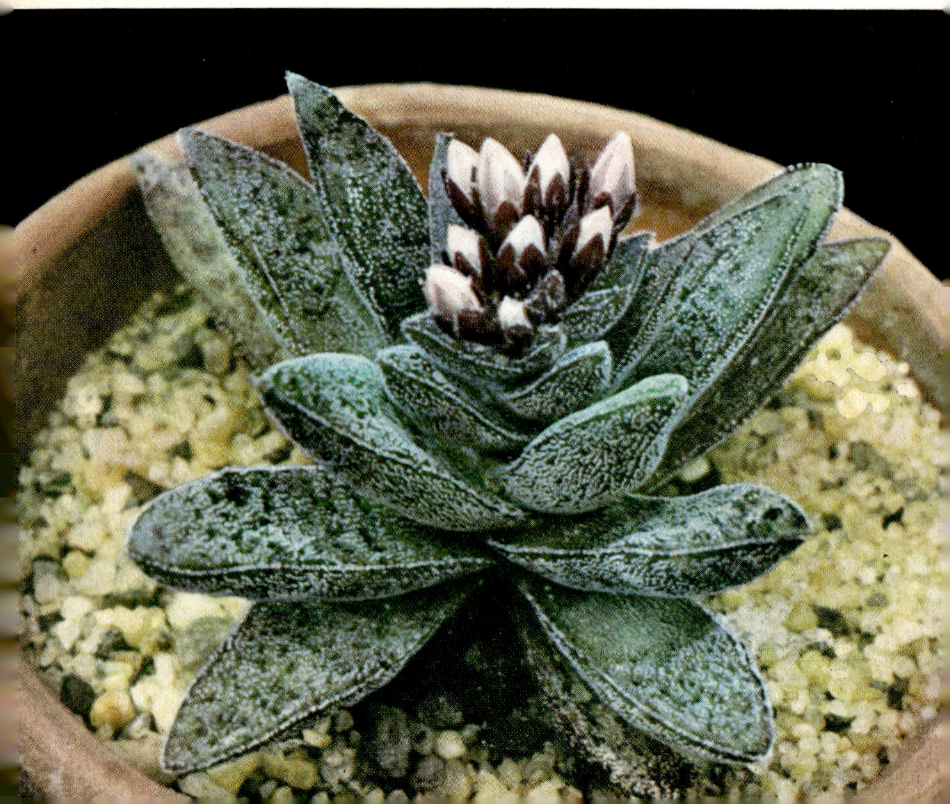

LXXXVII

Crassula gillii *Schonl.*

(S.W. Africa)

These species belong to the CRASSULA GROUP

NOTE: An easy growing, compact and free-flowering succulent often producing a mass of bloom quite early in the year. Plants measuring over 1 in. (2·54 cm) in diameter.

Rich leafmould soil, plenty of water and sun or slight shade give excellent results. Will stand dry winter cold, but if in a warmer position a little water may be necessary.

May be grown indoors also with success.

LXXXVIII

Crassula justus-corderoyi *Jacobs*

(S. Africa)

NOTE: Shown in a 2-in. (5 cm) pot, this attractive species produces its buds and flowers very slowly, the latter often remaining on the plant for many weeks, usually in late summer.

Cultivation as above.

Cotyledon grandiflora *Burm.*
(Cape Province)

COLOUR: Stems grey-brown tending to develop a papery surface which peels away from stems. Leaves (when present) bright green.

SIZE: The above is growing in a 3-in. (7·6 cm) pot.

NOTE: This is one of the deciduous group of succulents, the resting period being during spring and summer months when no more than light spraying should be applied.

During the growing season (autumn onwards), water freely but they require a slightly warmed greenhouse. A rich leafmould soil gives excellent growth, and flower spikes appear towards the end of the growing season.

Cotyledon hirtifolia *Barker*
(Cape Province)

COLOUR: Usually brownish, the old leaf bases being grey. Leaves (when present) light green and slightly sticky with velvety surface.

SIZE: Growing in a 3-in. (7·6 cm) pot.

NOTE: Another member of the deciduous group, requiring less water than average and rather more drainage—this is important. Treatment otherwise as for *C. grandiflora*.

CRASSULA GROUP

This genus offers a very wide variety of types, as can be seen from the half-tone photographs, and the two shown in colour.

All those I have included here can be grown in a small space. They can also be flowered in cultivation without difficulty, occurring at any season.

C. arta is one of the very slow-growing types. *C. barbata* and *C. trachysantha* are of the " very hairy " type, responding rather more quickly to ideal growing conditions.

C. nealeana has been in cultivation for many years under a variety of names but has only quite recently been officially named. *C. marnieriana* is a newer species, slow-growing and very colourful in sunny conditions.

Crassula arta *Schonl.*
(Little Namaqualand)

COLOUR: Usually silvery-grey, pale green on new growths.

SIZE: Shown enlarged about double size.

NOTE: One of the rarer and slower growing *Crassulas* liking a sandy open soil; much less water than average, but will stand dry cold quite well in winter.

Contrary to popular opinion, slight shade produces the best growths and a much healthier plant.

Crassula barbata *Thunb.*

(S. Africa)

COLOUR: Bright green with white hairs.

SIZE: Enlarged almost double usual size.

NOTE: A rich soil, some shade and plenty of water throughout all grow-ing months, will produce a fine plant with some branches.

In winter a little warmth is advised and slight water on mild days, this maintains a much better plant than when kept cold and dry during winter months.

Crassula marnieriana *Hbr. & Jcbn.*
(S.W. Africa)

COLOUR: Pale green with coral pink on leaf edges.

SIZE: Almost double natural size shown.

NOTE: One of the newer *Crassulas* to cultivation. Attractive form and colour. Note the aerial roots which form in odd positions along stems.

Shade is important for this species and quite free watering in warm weather. Slow growing, this plant needs good drainage and some warmth in winter.

K   465

Crassula nealeana *Higgins*
(S. Africa)

COLOUR: Chalky grey-green with reddish markings.

SIZE: About double actual size shown.

FLOWER: Creamy.

NOTE: A recently named species which has been in cultivation for many years (unnamed).

Easy culture, stands cold quite well. A rich soil and average water give excellent results. Larger plants as they group tend to trail or hang downwards.

Crassula trachysantha *Harv.*
(Cape Province)

COLOUR: Bright green with white hairy leaf surfaces.

SIZE: Approximately natural size shown.

NOTE: An attractive succulent, easy to grow under normal conditions. Plenty of water and a rich soil, with slight winter warmth, will produce good plants.

CYANOTIS

This genus contains many species. Very few, however, are so far in cultivation. Coming from tropical Africa, one would expect them to be difficult, this is not so as they have been found to withstand cold greenhouse conditions quite well.

Most species have hairy leaves and their flowers, although small, are really magnificent when examined closely, all being similar in form.

To illustrate the genus, I have included *Cyanotis somaliensis* (the best-known species in cultivation) in colour showing both plant and flower. (See page 506).

ECHEVERIA GROUP

One genus, extra to Volume I, now illustrated is *Dudleya*, noted for its pure white " mealy " surfaced leaves and slowness of growth, most species being comparatively dwarf in habit.

Echeveria gibbiflora var. *carunculata* is not common in collections and amongst the most " weird " in this genus, as can be seen from the half-tone photograph.

Pachyphytum viride is quite rare. This I illustrate in both half-tone and colour. Notable for its slow growth, it is however not difficult to cultivate and the wax-like flowers are produced on a " drooping " flower-spike.

Dudleya farinosa *B. & R.*
(California)

COLOUR: Almost entirely covered with a white mealy surface.

SIZE: About natural size shown.

NOTE: Slow growing, extra care with drainage is important, when average water may be applied.

In winter, some warmth is advised and the plant should be dry.

Not suited to indoor culture.

Echeveria gibbiflora var. carunculata *Hort.*
(Mexico)

COLOUR: Pink to pale ice-blue stems, leaves similar in colour, the carunculate parts being more blue.

SIZE: Shown at one-quarter actual size.

NOTE: This very attractive and uncommon variety is not a fast grower in pot cultivation, but responds well to freer root space and plenty of water, with a rich leafmould soil.

Leaves do not always have the raised markings when young, and this habit is variable.

Tall flower-spikes, similar in colour, with bell-like flowers produced with good healthy plants. Stands dry cold in winter.

Pachyphytum viride *Walther.*
(Mexico)

COLOUR: Grey-brown stems with green to yellow-brown leaves.

SIZE: Shown at half size.

NOTE: This slow growing and rare species will produce strong " banana-like " leaves in sun, varying in colour according to amount of light.

Less than average water at all times but will stand dry winter cold quite well.

Flower-spike producing magnificent " waxy " blooms often lasting 1–2 months.

See colour illustration for flower on page 563.

EUPHORBIA GROUP

Monadenium and *Jatropha* are two additional genera to be illustrated, which were not included in Volume I. Both are rare in collections, but they are not unduly difficult to cultivate so long as the greenhouse has some warmth in winter.

I have made a point of including in the photography a number of *Euphorbias* coming from Morocco, and also the Canary Islands, which have rarely been illustrated anywhere in the past.

Although some of these names often appear in collections, in nearly all instances I have found these to be incorrectly named—in particular: *E. beaumieriana*, *E. officinarum*, both from Morocco, and *E. handiensis* from a remote part of the Canary Isles. The true species, collected from their native habitats, are among the half-tone photographs. These can be taken as the true species as they were collected from the " type-localities ".

Some of the leafy type Canary Isles *Euphorbias* are now becoming better known to collectors, *E. atropurpurea* being an example.

Euphorbia hallii is one of the more recently named species, recognising the work of H. Hall, the actual discoverer of this fine plant. It is also worth mentioning that when this species is grown from seed, the young specimens but one year old are truly representative of the larger plant shown and are already developing the large swollen roots.

E. stellata can be regarded as one of the curious and slow-growing types, the very large roots requiring a lot of space. I have included a colour photograph of the tip of a flowering branch.

Euphorbia atropurpurea *Brouss.*
(Canary Islands)

COLOUR: Stems pale green or brownish, leaves pale green.

SIZE: Shown slightly reduced.

NOTE: A very beautiful species from the Canary Isles which may produce its deep purple-red flowers in spring and late summer.

Given a rich soil, plenty of water and warmth, this soon becomes a freely branched, bush. In pots, they remain smaller and growth is much restricted. Stands dry winter cold well.

Euphorbia beaumieriana *L.*
(S. Morocco)

COLOUR: Deep glossy green with paler markings between ribs and grey thorns, the newer ones being deep brown.

SIZE: Slightly reduced.

NOTE: The true species is rarely found in collections today, although plants may have this name.

Slow growing, with great age becomes a much branched and spiny *Euphorbia*.

Dry and cold in winter does this plant no harm; it will also stand great summer heat.

Water freely when growing.

Euphorbia beaumieriana *L.*
(S. Morocco)

Part of a larger grouped specimen showing the erect stems and horny ribs developed with age.

See page 475.

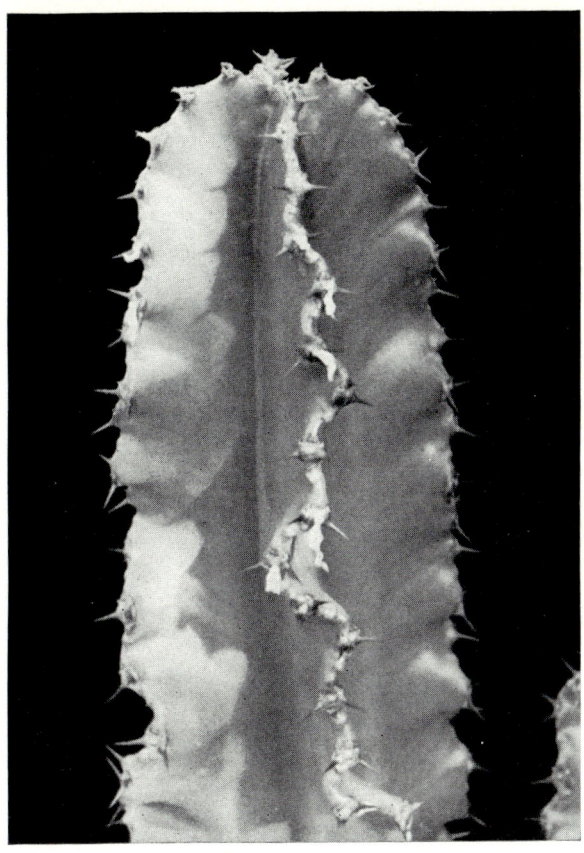

Euphorbia candelabrum var. erythraeae *Bgr.*
(Eritrea)

COLOUR: Bright green. Leaves, when present, also green. Thorns brown.

SIZE: Top of plant shown measures about 3 in. (7·6 cm) across.

NOTE: Tall growing, and if given a rich soil, plenty of water and warmth, a tall specimen can be obtained within a few years.

In winter some warmth is essential and the plant should be quite dry.

477

Euphorbia cereiformis *L.*

(Unknown)

COLOUR: Dull green becoming brown at base with age. Thorns mostly brown-grey, red on growing tips.

SIZE: This group is growing in a 9-in. (22·9 cm) pot.

FLOWER: Small purple-brown.

NOTE: This popular species can be grown indoors, in the table-garden or greenhouse. Small plants flower freely, even the single stem producing its quota of bloom.

Stands dry cold quite well, but in summer it likes plenty of water and a really good soil.

Euphorbia fasciculata *Thunb.*

(S. Africa)

COLOUR: Deep blue-green body, the thorny remains of old flower stalks being woody and grey.

SIZE: Shown slightly reduced.

NOTE: Very slow growing, this deep-rooted plant is rare in collections today. It requires very open and well-drained soil, much less than average water at all times. Dry cold does not harm these plants but a dry atmosphere is essential, thus very slight winter warmth is to be preferred.

479

Euphorbia ferox *Marloth.*
(Cape Province)

COLOUR: Pale blue-green stems with red-brown thorns, greying with age. Growing tips of stems produce small green leaves which rapidly turn bright red and remain for some weeks.

SIZE: This plant is shown at $\frac{1}{3}$ natural size.

NOTE: Not a fast grower, this species is variable, being one of the taller growing forms of this *Euphorbia*.

Average to rather less water, stands cold when dry in winter.

Euphorbia flanaganii fa. cristata *Hort.*
(Cape Province)

COLOUR: Bright shiny green.

SIZE: Shown slightly reduced.

NOTE: Many plants in collections go under the wrong name of *E. caput-medusae-v. cristata.*

This easy-growing species likes water and some shade to attain its finest proportions. Slight winter warmth is advised, when a little water may be necessary.

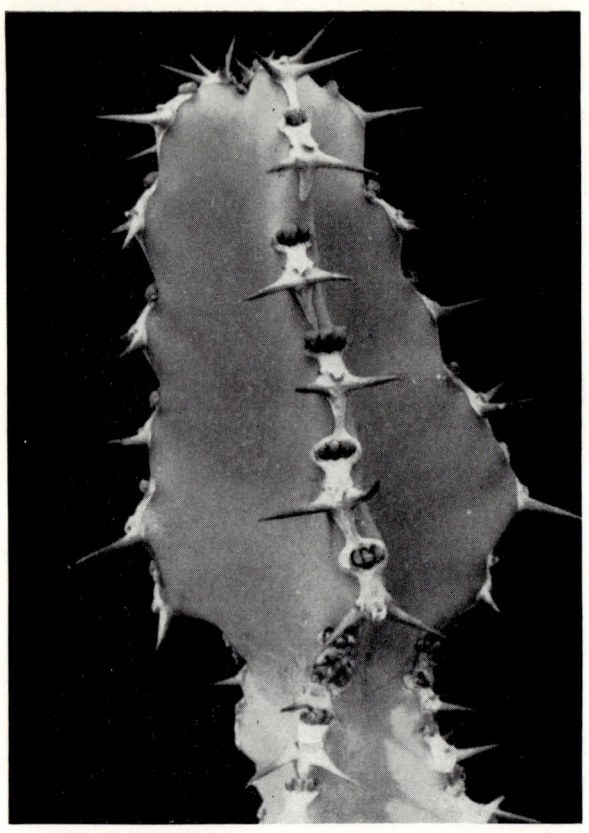

Euphorbia franckiana *Berger.*
(South Africa)

COLOUR: Bright green with white thorns, brown tipped.

SIZE: Very slightly enlarged.

NOTE: An easy plant to grow, stands cold quite well but is not a fast grower.

Water rather less than average except when growing and in hot weather, otherwise normal leafmould soil.

Euphorbia hallii *Dyer.*
(Cape Province)

COLOUR: Pale green body with darker green thin leaves becoming red-tinted in autumn.

SIZE: Natural size shown.

NOTE: A deep tuberous-rooted species requiring a large, deep pot. Water less than average at all times, keep slightly warmer in winter.

One of the more recently named species, not common in collections.

Euphorbia handiensis *Burch.*

(Canary Islands)

COLOUR: Very light green with chalky, horny markings, particularly on older growths.

SIZE: Shown slightly reduced.

NOTE: Very rare species, the true species being extremely rare in collections today.

A very open sandy soil, this plant requires much less than average amounts of water and slight winter warmth is considered essential.

Euphorbia ledienii *Berger.*
(Cape Province)

COLOUR: Deep green stems with dark brown thorns.

SIZE: Natural size shown.

FLOWER: Bright yellow.

NOTE: Fairly fast growing and easy to flower in late spring or summer.

A rich soil, plenty of water when in growth and normal dry cold in winter does not seem to do any harm.

This species is noted for its habit in producing its many flowers a long way down the stems; with a branched specimen, it is a fine sight.

Euphorbia officinarum *L.*

(Morocco)

COLOUR: Deep green with whitish spines forming almost a continuous rib. Spines usually brown-tipped. Lower part of plant grey.

SIZE: The main stem measures $2\frac{1}{2}$ in. (6·3 cm) in diameter.

NOTE: Slow growing, very sturdy plant which will stand dry cold in winter.

Requires much less than average water, and special care in drainage with a good sandy soil.

Euphorbia pentops *W.D.S.*
(Cape Province)

COLOUR: Light green with slight mottling, brown at old leaf bases
Leaves near growing tips (when present) also light green.

SIZE: Actual size shown.

NOTE: Slow growing deep-rooted species requiring a fairly large and
deep pot with very special care being taken in the drainage. The plant
must not be over-watered at any time. Keep dry in winter.

Not suited to indoor culture.

Euphorbia pteroneura *Bgr.*
(Mexico)

COLOUR: Dull green stems, paler at angles. Green leaves, edged red.

SIZE: Actual size shown.

NOTE: Requires much warmer winter conditions, with slight watering. In summer months it likes plenty of water and a rich soil.

Fairly quick growing, forming into clusters of stems. Not common in collections today.

Euphorbia regis-jubae *W. & B.*
(Canary Islands)

COLOUR: Green to grey stems, with pale green leaves.

SIZE: Plant shown at about a quarter that photographed, but
mature and much larger plants do develop thicker stems
with age.

NOTE: Plenty of water, a rich soil, this plant does well, producing many
small yellow-green flowers at almost any time of year.

It stands cold very well, even when not completely dry at the root. Very
old stems become covered with an almost " corky " covering.

Euphorbia stapelioides *Boiss.*
(S. Africa)

COLOUR: Pale blue-green stems, brown at possible branching positions

SIZE: Very slightly enlarged.

NOTE: A deep-rooted species requiring a large pot, good drainage and rather more sand than many; water with care at all times.

Slight warmth in winter is advised for this dwarf-growing uncommon species.

Euphorbia stellata   *Willd.*
(Cape Province)

COLOUR: Very bright green stems, twisting into odd contortions with brown to greyish thorns.

SIZE: Growing in a 4½-in. (11·4 cm) pot.

FLOWER: See colour illustration on page 451.

NOTE: This species has very large, twisted and tuberous roots, its stems growing prostrate or semi-erect. Very slow indeed and its watering needs are rather small. Very free-flowering.

Will stand dry cold, but slight warmth maintains a better plant.

Euphorbia susannae *Marloth.*
(Cape Province)

COLOUR: Deep green, brownish on lower parts of old stems.

SIZE: Slightly enlarged.

NOTE: Very slow growing, gradually becoming clustered with tightly compact branches forming from the base. A variable species, some being much more dwarf in habit than the plant illustrated.

Keep free of winter cold, quite dry during all cold months and water in summer, with care at all times. Very sandy soil advised.

Not suited to indoor culture.

Jatropha podagrica *Hook.*
(Panama)

COLOUR: Rough surfaced, greyish stems with brown and green stipules. (Shown near top of stem.) Leaves green on upper surface, paler beneath. New leaves shiny reddish-brown.

SIZE: Actual size shown of plant photographed.

NOTE: Requires warmer treatment in winter (not below 50° F (10° C)), with a little water, even when without its leaves. As new leaves begin to appear in spring, increasing amounts of water should be given.

This plant prefers a soil of leafmould and sand only.

Monadenium lugardae *N.E. Br.*
(Bechuanaland)

COLOUR: Bright green leaves with a rough surface and stems a similar green.

SIZE: Actual size shown of plant photographed.

NOTE: Not difficult, provided some winter warmth is given, when a little water is advised.

Increase water (in summer months) when plants show growth of more leaves.

Flowers when produced in late autumn are small pale greenish-yellow, tinted pink and appearing from between leaves.

494

Monadenium lugardae *N.E. Br.*
(Bechuanaland)

Much enlarged close-up of the top of plant showing flowers in greater detail.

See also page 494.

GASTERIA

To illustrate just one of this genus, I have included *G. neliana* as an example of a much smaller, slow-growing species with its round-ended leaves contrasting with *G. verrucosa* as shown in Volume I.

All *Gasterias* I have grown seem capable of withstanding quite cold winter conditions and few, if any, need be regarded as difficult in any way.

HALF-TONE PLATE
Illustrated in Volume I

Gasteria verrucosa   228

Gasteria neliana *V. Poelln.*

(L. Namaqualand)

COLOUR: Dull rather dark green leaves with pale green markings and edges.

SIZE: Actual size shown.

NOTE: Slow growing, a well-drained soil and much less than average water at all times.

This species does best in broken sunlight.

Cold dry winter treatment does no harm, otherwise normal treatment in water, etc.

HAWORTHIA GROUP

Plants coming under the genus *Astroloba* were, until recent years, known as " *Apicra* ". All have very sharp-pointed leaves and although with age they form dense clumps, they are quite slow of growth, being ideal for the small greenhouse especially as they prefer some shade. The under-staging position suiting them well.

The two *Haworthias* shown give some idea of the distinctive forms which occur.

Astroloba deltoidea *Baker*
(Cape Province)

COLOUR: Bright, shiny green leaves with a very sharp point.

SIZE: Slightly enlarged.

NOTE: Slow growing, requiring less than average water. Best grown in a slightly shaded position.

Rich soil but good drainage important, stands winter dry cold well.

Astroloba pentagona *Willd.*
(Cape Province)

COLOUR: Bright green with paler raised markings.

SIZE: Slightly enlarged.

NOTE: Another slow-growing species which branches at or below soil level to form a compact cluster.

Dry cold in winter, less than average water at all times.

Haworthia bolusii *Bak.*
(Cape Province)

COLOUR: Very pale green translucent leaves with olive-green toward leaf tips and white hairy margins.

SIZE: Slightly enlarged.

NOTE: One of the finest species in this genus, requiring a well-drained soil, less than average water and broken sunlight in order to produce the finest specimens.

In winter, complete dryness is important, when the rosette will tend to close towards the centre for the resting period. Slight warmth is advised but not essential.

501

Haworthia fasciata *Haw.*
(S. Africa)

COLOUR: Deep green, often bronzed with pure white raised markings.

SIZE: Actual size or slightly reduced.

NOTE: This attractive species is easy to cultivate. May be grown on window-ledge with good results as slight broken sunlight gives best results.

Water about average. It will stand dry cold in winter without harm.

502

IDRIA

Idria columnaris is perhaps one of the oddest of succulents, often compared in appearance to an inverted carrot or other similar root vegetable.

Specimens of any size are extremely rare in collections, but small, young plants are seen as they are not difficult to raise from seed, and even at this stage closely resemble adult specimens.

In habitat, these plants do eventually reach a height of some 30–40 ft., (9.12 cm), occasionally with an odd branch. Being of very slow growth these tall plants must be of very great age.

Idria columnaris *Klgg.*
(Lower California)

COLOUR: Olive-green to brown, and grey with age. Leaves green.

SIZE: The above is growing in a 12-in. (30·5 cm) pot.

NOTE: Rare in collections as large and old specimens (shown above). Likes a rich soil and plenty of water when it produces a large head of thorny branches and leaves.

If very dry, leaves drop off but are soon produced again with growing conditions.

Does not have a definite resting period.

KALANCHOE

Most of the plants coming within this group are easy of culture, the beauty being most noticeable in their beautiful leaves, which differ in type from one species to another.

The finest plants are those where slight winter warmth is possible in the greenhouse as the colourful and often quite large and well-developed heads can be maintained by this means. If allowed to become too cold, they may lose much of their size.

Five species, one in colour, I have used to illustrate the varied leaf forms. *Bryophyllum*, coming within this group, is usually found to produce a few " plantlets " on its leaves at times. The true *Kalanchoe* does not have this characteristic.

The *Kalanchoe* sometimes produces new plantlets on the old flower-pikes as an added means of reproduction.

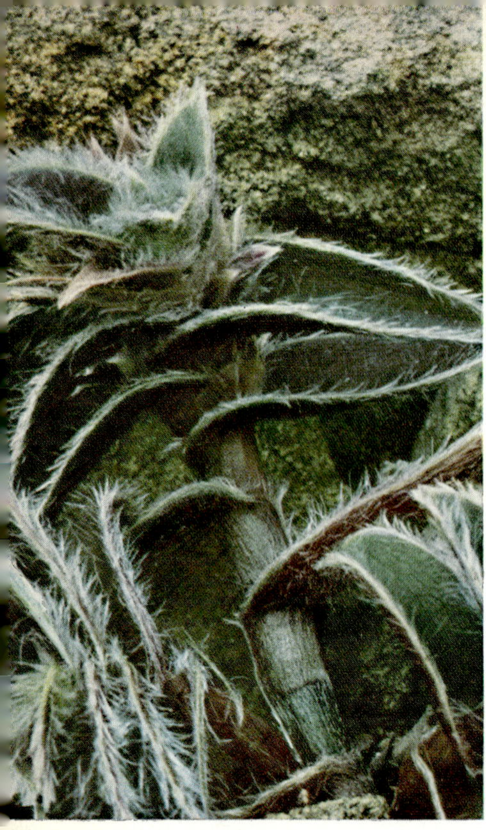
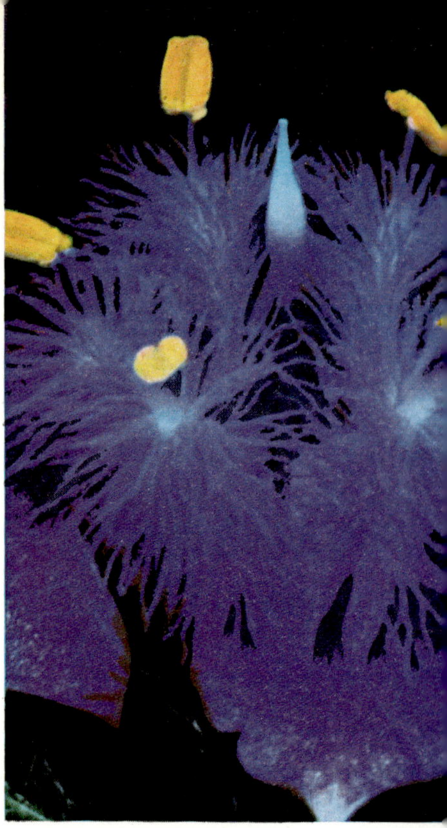
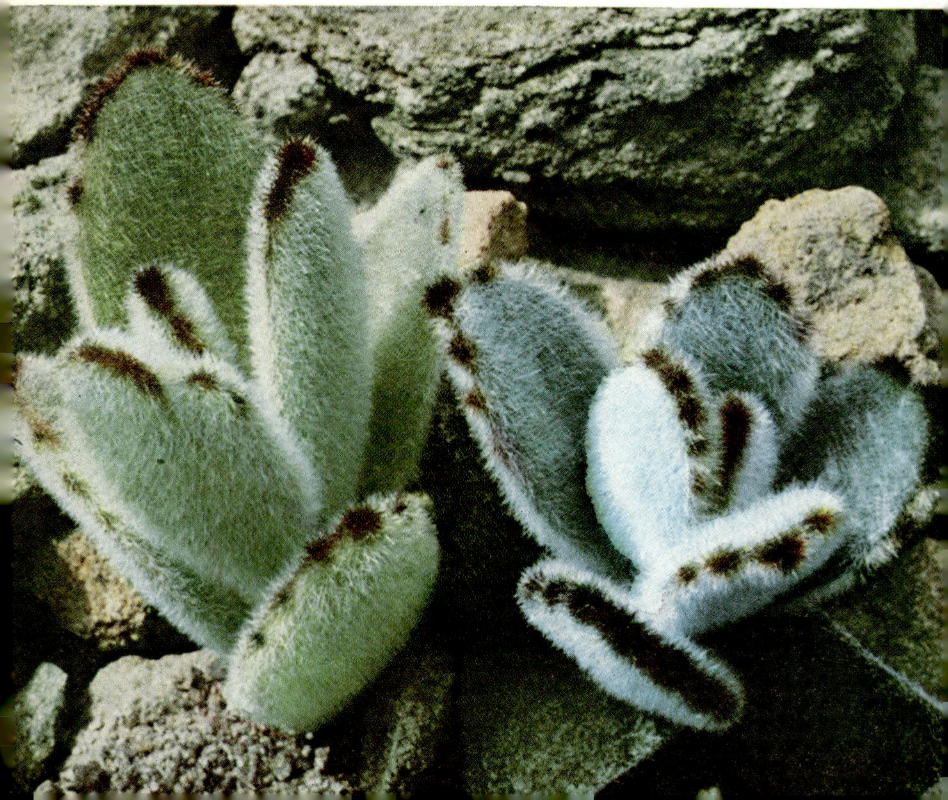

Top left and
Top right

LXXXIX *This species belongs to the* CYANOTIS GROUP

Cyanotis somaliensis *C. B. Clarke*

(Somaliland)

NOTE: An attractive hairy succulent, requiring rich soil and plenty of water, when it will produce many flowers which open for a few hours only during morning, each " plume-like " flower measuring barely ⅓ in. (0·8 cm), but very beautiful when viewed under a pocket-lens.

The " much-enlarged " illustration shows clearly the delicate beauty of this " short-lived " flower, but plants produce their flowers throughout the growing season.

See also page 468.

Bottom

XC *This species belongs to the* KALANCHOE GROUP

Kalanchoe tomentosa *Bak.*

(Madagascar)

NOTE: These very beautiful plants are shown as young specimens each measuring about 1½–2 in. (3·8–5 cm) across. The size may increase with age to perhaps 6 in. (15 cm) across, a stem developing over a few years of growth.

Slight winter warmth is advised, otherwise the plant may lose its leaves. Water fairly freely in warm weather.

Bryophyllum crenatum *Bak.*
(Tropical Africa)

COLOUR: Pink stems, pale blue leaves with a red edge.

SIZE: Shown at twice normal size.

NOTE: Another attractive but lesser known species responding well to a rich soil and plenty of water during warm weather. Slight water and warmth in winter advised.

Produces a few " plantlets " on leaf edges at times, more often on slow growing specimens.

Kalanchoe beharensis *Drake*
(Madagascar)

COLOUR: Greenish-brown stems, rather masked by the white velvety surface. Leaves also velvety, olive-green to brown.

SIZE: Shown about a quarter of its natural size.

NOTE: This very beautiful succulent has many leaf forms, some being entirely brown on upper surface, pale green underneath.

Requiring a very rich leafmould soil, plenty of water in all warm months. In winter it should have some warmth and a little water to maintain its beautiful head of leaves.

If kept too cool and dry, many of the leaves will be lost.

Kalanchoe longiflora var. coccinea *Mnr.*

(Tropical Africa)

COLOUR: Stems bronze-red, leaves varying between deep green and bronze-red.

SIZE: Slightly reduced.

NOTE: An attractive succulent for its leaf colour. It also produces bright yellow flowers on a tall spike, usually in winter.

This *Kalanchoe* is not so subject to cold as many, but slight warmth in winter is advised. A rich soil gives finest leaves.

N.B. This variety has previously been in cultivation for very many years as *K. crenata.*

Kalanchoe humbertii *Guill.*

(Madagascar)

COLOUR: Very pale green stems with leaves of similar colour and a red edge.

SIZE: Top of plant shown at twice actual size.

NOTE: This compact-growing, rather attractive succulent, likes a rich soil, plenty of water in summer months, very little in winter when in slightly warmed greenhouse. Will stand cold but may drop leaves if dry for too long.

Flowers pale, pinkish, of " waxy " bell-like appearance and usually appearing very late in autumn or even in winter.

KLEINIA

As mentioned in Volume I, *Kleinia* and *Senecio* are very similar. Some authorities consider that they should all be under the genus heading of *Senecio*.

Five species of *Kleinia* were illustrated in Volume I. I am therefore excluding further additions under this heading and including instead three additional true species of *Senecio*.

HALF-TONE PLATES
Illustrated in Volume I

(= Senecio anteuphorbium)
(= Senecio articulatus)

MESEMBRYANTHEMUM GROUP

To illustrate this very wide group, most of which can be classed as among the dwarf types, I have included eleven photographs, eight of which are in colour.

The following eight genera are additional to those shown in Volume I: *Conophyllum, Kensitia, Monilaria, Nananthus, Neohenricia, Ophthalmophyllum, Pleiospilos* and *Rhinephyllum.*

A characteristic of this group is that so many of the dwarf species possess beautifully marked leaves, often with almost " embossed " leaf patterns.

Nearly all are free-flowering and most will stand a certain amount of quite cold winter weather without harm—a point not generally realised. One section in my collection has a good representative selection of the various types growing in a bed near to the glass at ground level, where outside rain and even melted snow provide moisture to their roots.

Top

XCI *These species belong to the* MESEMBRYANTHEMUM GROUP

Conophytum bicarinatum *L. Bol.*
(Cape Province)

NOTE: Less common in collections, this species is nicely marked on edges, and is free-flowering during late summer and autumn.

A leafmould soil with gritty sand to ensure good drainage, and normal watering from about June onwards. The dry period should usually be for the months of April, May and perhaps a part of June, unless growth is already showing by splits in the old dried covering.

A light spraying to form a " mist " is often beneficial during the " dry period ".

Bottom

XCII

Conophytum luckhoffii *Lavis.*
(Cape Province)

NOTE: A much more dwarfed species, well marked on plant bodies forming into large clusters.

Cultivation as for above.

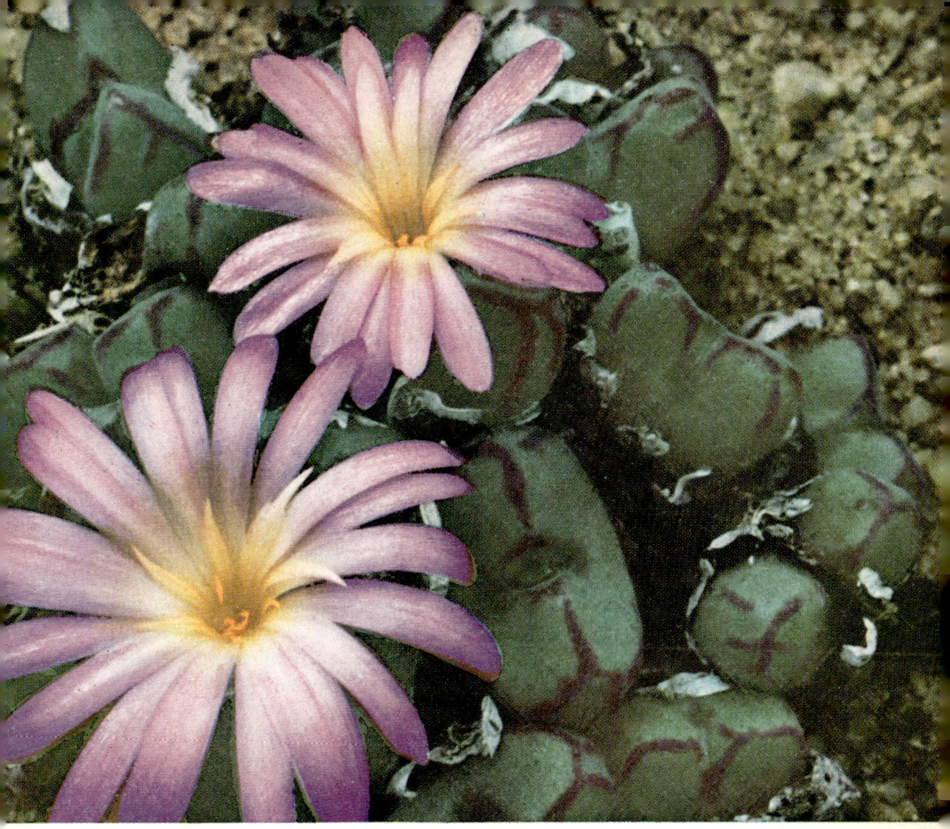

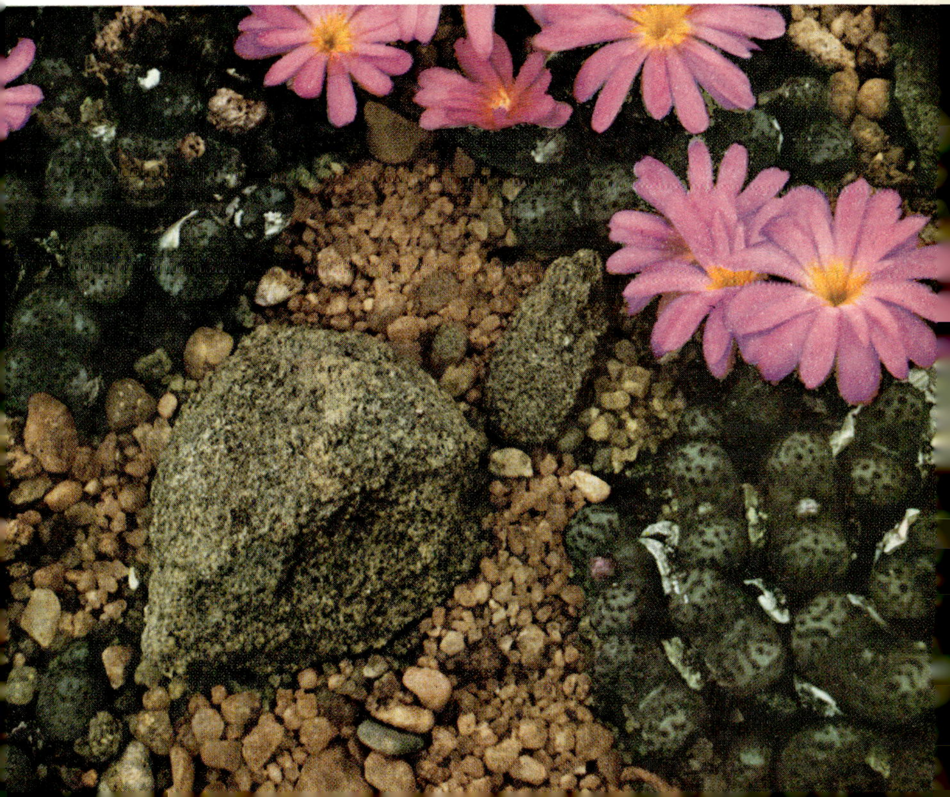

These species belong to the MESEMBRYANTHEMUM GROUP

Argyroderma ovale *L. Bol.*

(Cape Province)

NOTE: The plants pictured are growing in a 6-in. (15 cm) pan. Buds form very slowly and flowering extends over many weeks during the latter part of the year.

Easy culture, will stand dry cold quite well but in summer, when plants are seen to be growing, care should be taken not to over-water as this may split the body of the plant.

After flowering has ended, they should be rested with little more than " mist spraying ".

Bottom
XCIV

(Cape Province)

NOTE: Easy growing, likes plenty of water throughout all growing months from spring until late autumn.

Kept dry in coldest winter months, it will stand cold. A fairly large pot or planted in a bed enables trailing stems to root down when stems re-branch at many positions.

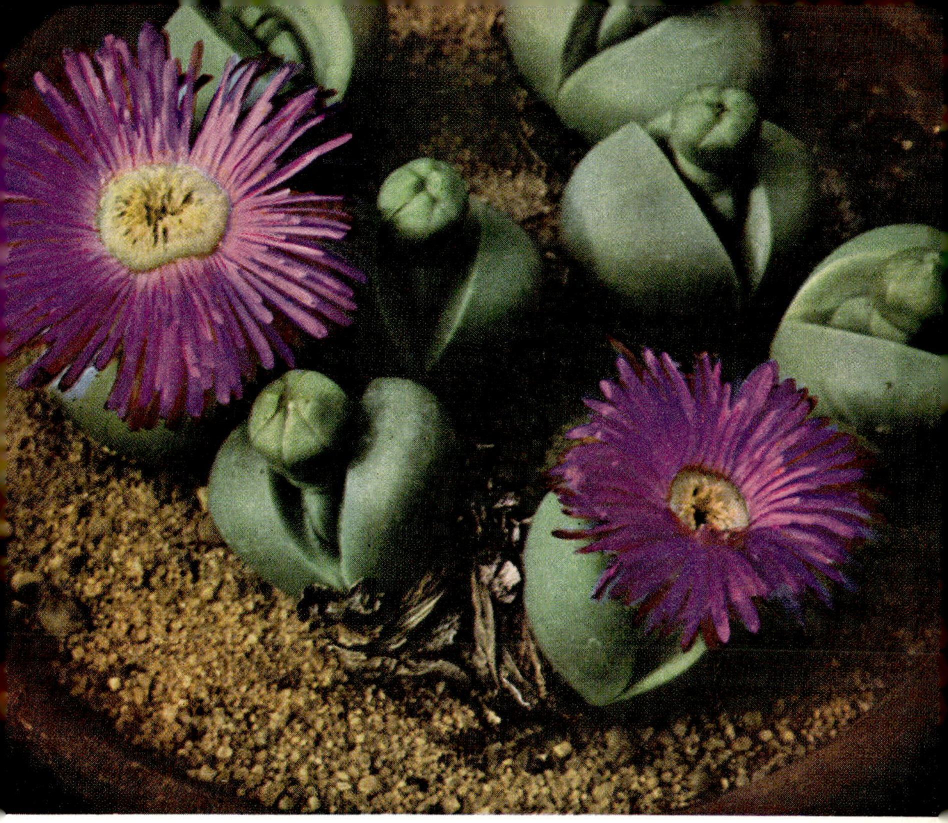

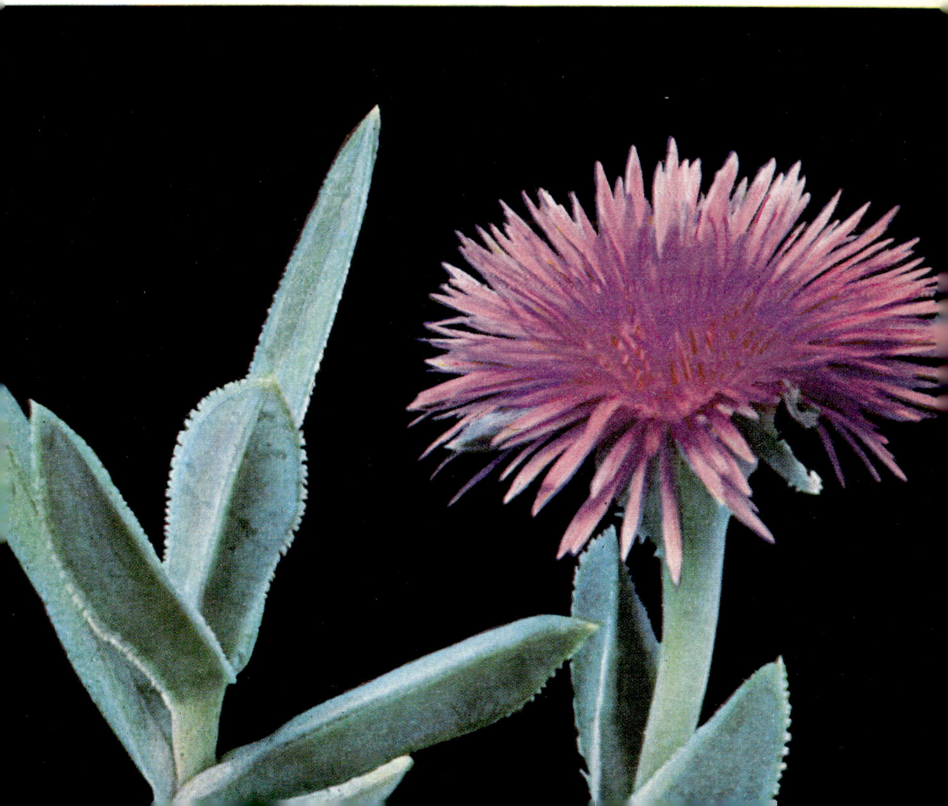

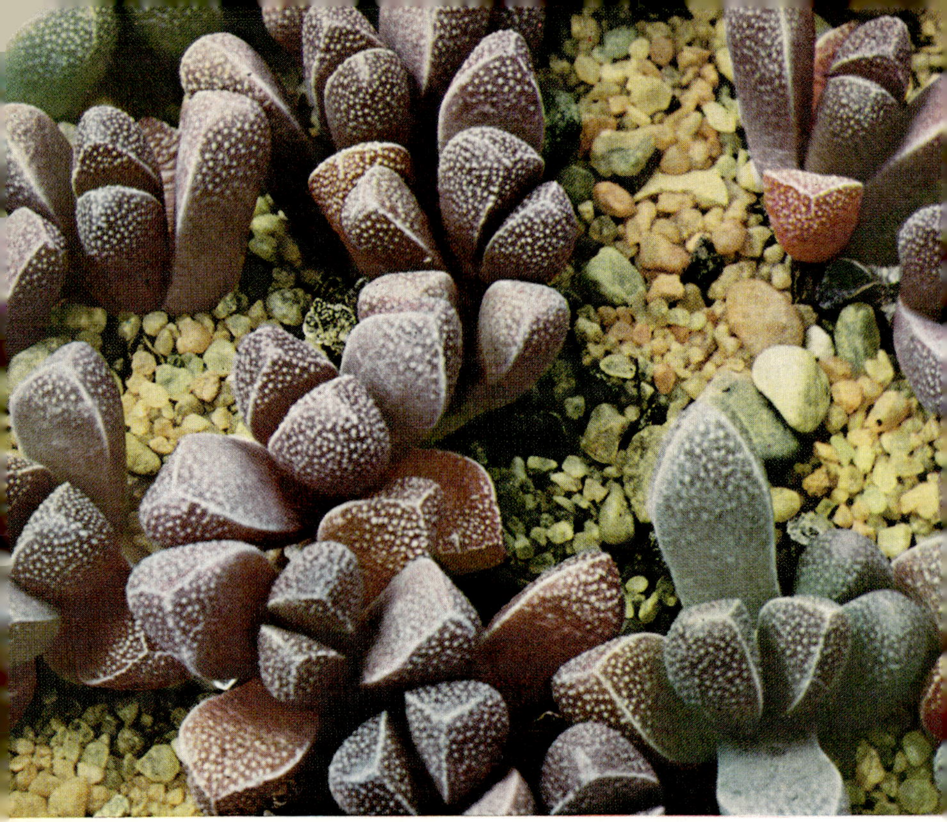

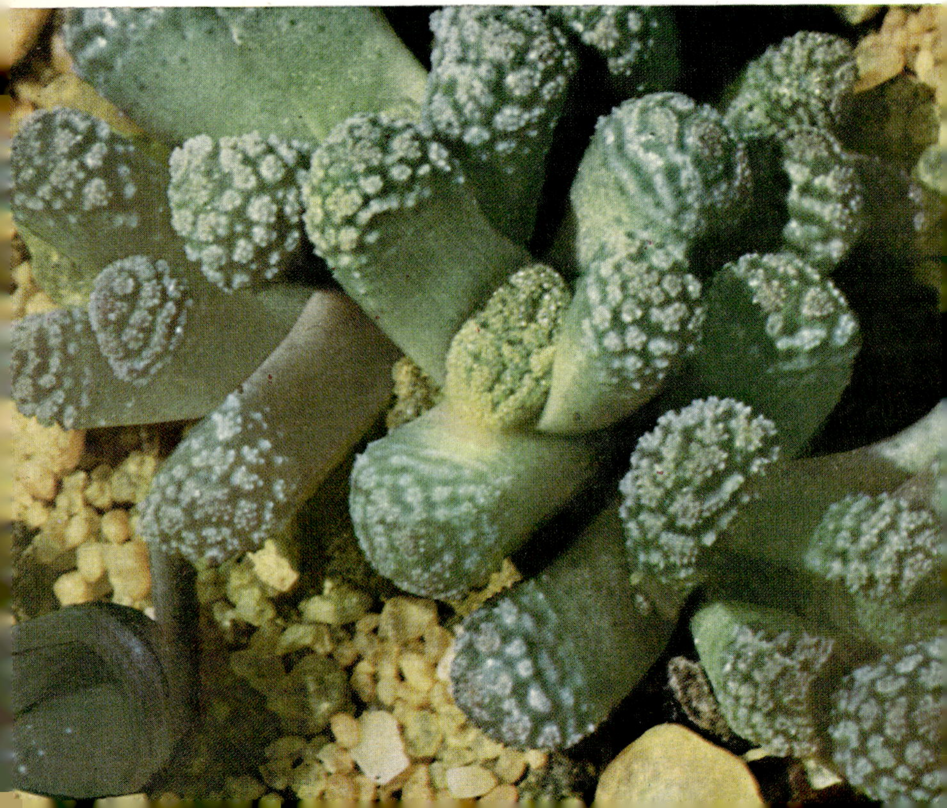

XCV *These species belong to the* MESEMBRYANTHEMUM GROUP

Rhinephyllum muiri *N.E. Br.*
(Cape Province)

NOTE: A very attractive and well-marked species, each head of leaves being barely 1 in. (2·54 cm) across.

Requires a rather deep pot as roots are thickened well below soil level. Average water with dry winter period, when it stands cold quite well.

XCVI

Neohenricia sibbetii *L. Bol.*
(Orange Free State)

NOTE: A very low growing species, eventually grouping. Leaf tips are beautifully marked, as will be seen in the illustration.

Extra well-drained soil and less water than average at all times with only " mist " spraying after flowering has ended. Slight winter warmth is essential.

Conophyllum globosum *L. Bol.*
(L. Namaqualand)

COLOUR: Pale green with a slightly glandular surface. Leaves (when present) bright green, glandular and glistening in sunlight.

SIZE: Almost twice normal size shown.

NOTE: Slow growing and having its resting period in summer when only slight mist-spraying is necessary. With signs of growth in autumn, some extra water should be given but always in moderation.

Very sandy soil necessary for this plant. Slight winter warmth advised as plant may not have finished growing.

Monilaria moniliformis *Schwant.*

(L. Namaqualand)

COLOUR: Olive-brown stems, green when new. Leaves (when present) bright green, glandular and glistening in sunlight.

SIZE: Natural size shown.

NOTE: Very rare in collections, this plant must be kept dry throughout the summer when without its leaves (except for slight mist spraying at intervals of several weeks).

In autumn, when leaves begin to appear, increase amount of water gradually and until leaves turn yellowish, prior to growing period ending

Must be kept in a warm winter position.

Nananthus malherbei *Schwant.*
(S. Africa)

COLOUR: Dull green leaves with pale green to white markings.

SIZE: Slightly enlarged.

FLOWER: Peach-coloured.

NOTE: This handsome dwarf *Mesembryanthemum* is quite easy to grow and flowers in autumn or earlier.

Good soil, about average water, these grow exceptionally well in sandy leafmould.

Slight winter warmth is advised.

SEMPERVIVUM GROUP

In Volume I, *Aeonium tabulaeforme* was the only representative of this group which also contains the following additional genera: *Aichryson*, *Greenovia*, and *Monanthes*.

All four genera are now illustrated in this volume, including one species of each in colour.

Three species recently named by E. Sventenius, who has made a great study of the Canarian Flora, are illustrated in half-tone photographs, these being: *Aeonium rubrolineatum*, *Monanthes adenoscepes*, and *Monanthes niphophila*.

It is a common fallacy that when a plant of this group flowers it dies completely. In actual fact, this is true of only a few species and even these perpetuate themselves by producing branches, usually just prior to flowering, as for instance with *Greenovia aurea*.

Of the shrubby types, these usually divide into two or more heads after flowering.

HALF-TONE PLATE
Illustrated in Volume I
Aeonium tabulaeforme   273

Aeonium arboreum *W. & B.*
(S.W. and N. Morocco)

COLOUR: Brownish green stems with bright green leaves, sometimes marked with purple nearer the tips of leaves.

SIZE: Plant photographed at just under half-size.

NOTE: Very popular for use as outside summer decoration in large pots or tubs, when the leaves take on some fine colouring and grow very compact. In winter they may be housed in a cool greenhouse and kept dry but slight protection against frost is advised.

Grown in greenhouse at all times, leaves may be larger and require more water.

Aeonium lindleyi *W. & B.*
(Canary Islands)

COLOUR: Whitish-brown stems with bright green and sticky leaves.

SIZE: Actual size shown.

NOTE: This attractive little species normally grows its heads as shown in the above photograph. It is dwarf in habit, preferring a slightly shady position and most water during winter and spring, when slight warmth should be given.

Normal rich soil suits this plant.

XCVII   *These species belong to the* MESEMBRYANTHEMUM GROUP

Ophthalmophyllum pillansii *L. Bol.*
(S. Africa)

NOTE: An attractive plant to have in any collection. Slow to group, often single plants remain for some years before increasing.

Treatment as for *Lithops*.

Bottom

XCVIII

Pleiospilos nelii *Schwant.*
(S. Africa)

NOTE: Each plant pictured measures about 2 in. (5 cm) across. Growth is, slower than with many others in this genus but flowers regularly each year the actual flowering time varying considerably according to season.

Less than average water at all times and when growth is ended after flowering in particular, slight " mist " spraying is all this species requires. Keep dry in winter.

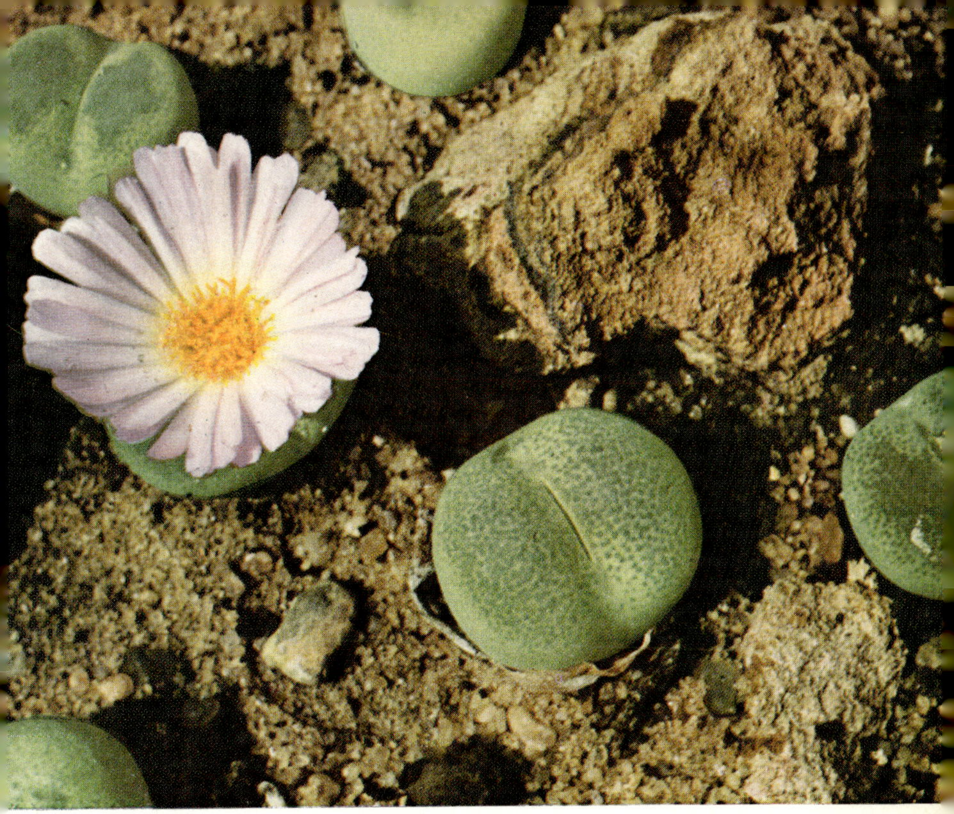

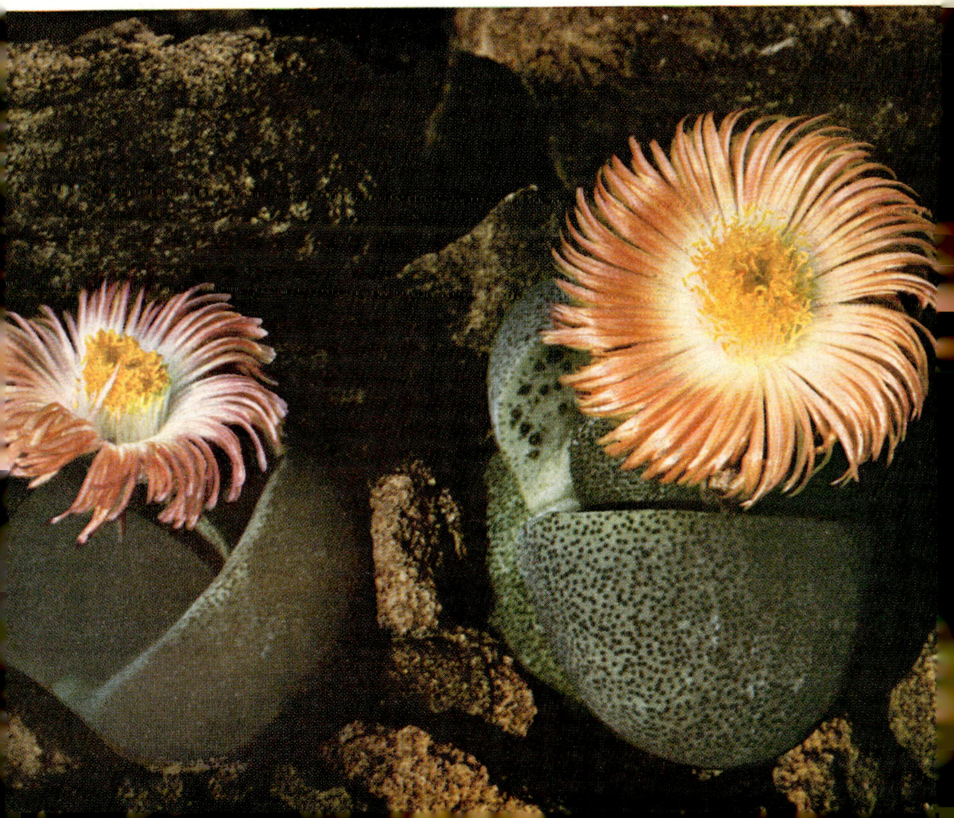

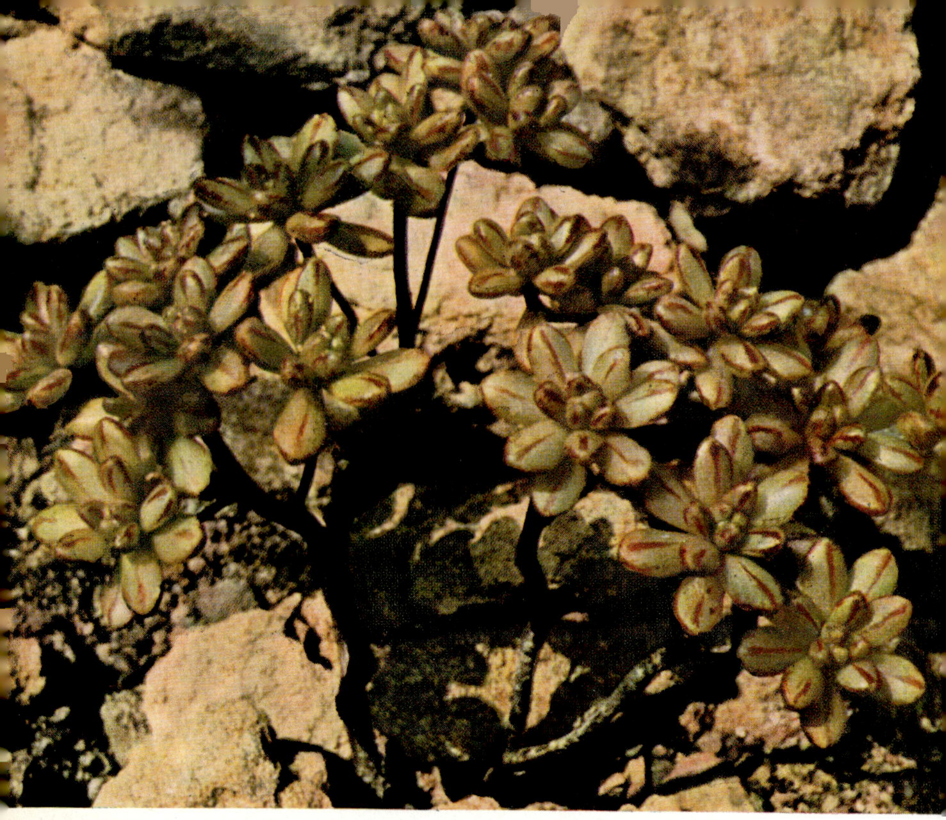

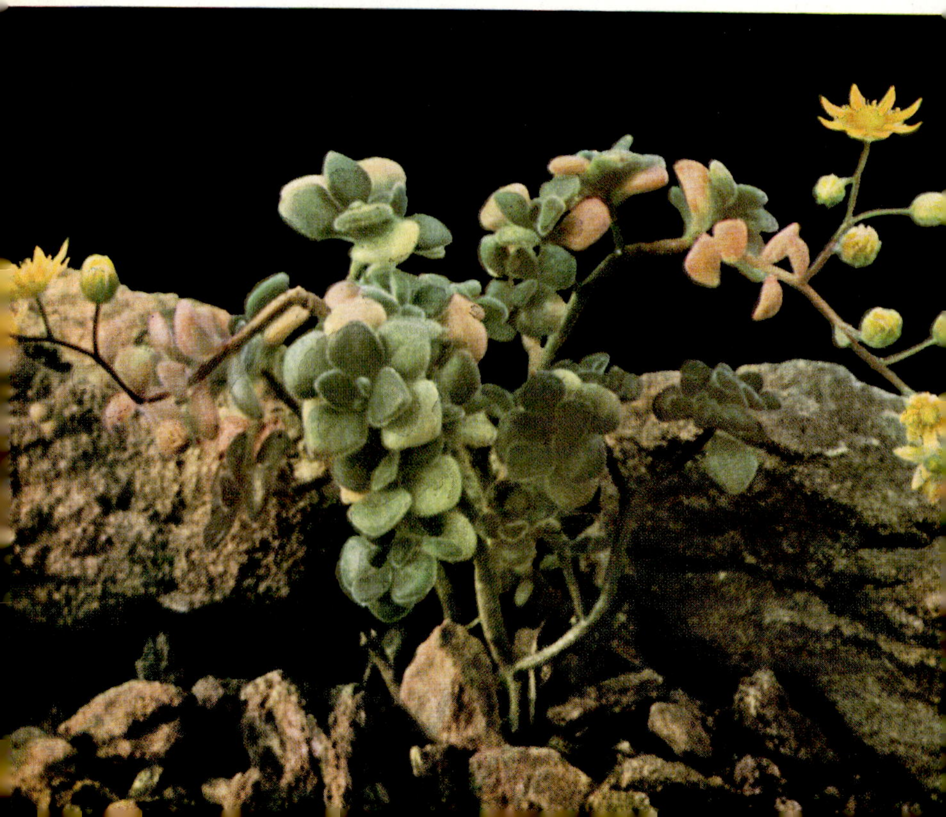

These species belong to the SEMPERVIVUM GROUP

Aeonium sedifolium *Ptd. & Pst.*
(Canary Islands)

NOTE: Forms a miniature tree up to about 6 in. (15 cm) with mature plants. The illustration is of one 3 in. (7·6 cm) tall. Leaves slightly "sticky".

Water from late summer to early spring with slight winter warmth advised, " Mist " or light watering only during other months. Free-flowering and of easy culture.

Bottom
C

Aichryson dichotomum *W. & B.*
(Canary Islands)

NOTE: Another tree-like, small growing species requiring much the same treatment as above.

Outer branches will root themselves down, thus forming a grouped specimen of increasing size.

Aeonium rubrolineatum *Svent.*
(Canary Islands)

COLOUR: White to brown stems. Bright green leaves marked with purple, leaves having a pale pink hairy edge.

SIZE: Actual size of plant photographed.

NOTE: One of the newer species to cultivation, an attractive form of easy culture and requiring most water during winter and spring, when a large head of leaves may be produced.

In summer when resting, the head of leaves becomes greatly diminished.

Slight warmth in winter is advised.

Aeonium smithii *W. & B.*
(Canary Islands)

COLOUR: Stems covered in white hairs, greyish-brown. Bright green leaves with darker markings on the under surfaces.

SIZE: Shown slightly enlarged.

NOTE: An unusual *Aeonium* of dwarf habit; from a high altitude yet is sensitive to cold, often losing its leaves unless kept in some winter warmth. If quite cold in winter, the stems may bear no leaves at all, yet re-grow them the following autumn. To maintain this plant in its best conditions, water in autumn and winter, keep protected from frost and give slight waterings at intervals in resting period.

Flowers golden-yellow in late winter.

Aeonium undulatum *W. & B.*
(Canary Islands)

COLOUR: Stems white-grey, leaves a shiny but light green with a pale pink edge.

SIZE: Actual size of plant photographed.

NOTE: Normal treatment as for most other *Aeoniums*, producing its largest head of " undulated " leaves during the winter and spring.

Heads diminish in size during the resting period.

Greenovia aurea *W. & B.*
(Canary Islands)

COLOUR: Pastel blue-green, often becoming very pink in summer when resting.

SIZE: Slightly reduced.

FLOWER: See colour illustration on page 535.

NOTE: The plant shown is in its resting state; towards autumn when more water can be given, the rosettes open out and flowering may follow. The main head dies after flowering, being replaced by one or more small branches.

Provided the rosette is quite dry, it will stand winter cold. It has been known to stand several degrees of frost.

These species belong to the SEMPERVIVUM GROUP

Greenovia aurea *W. & B.*
(Canary Islands)

See page 533 for Notes on this species.

Monanthes muralis *Christ.*
(Canary Islands)

NOTE: A very beautiful little plant with its many " star-like " flowers is seen growing in a 2-in. (5 cm) pot.

Flowers during late winter and early spring for a long period.

Slightly less than average water for this species, and " mist " spraying only during summer months.

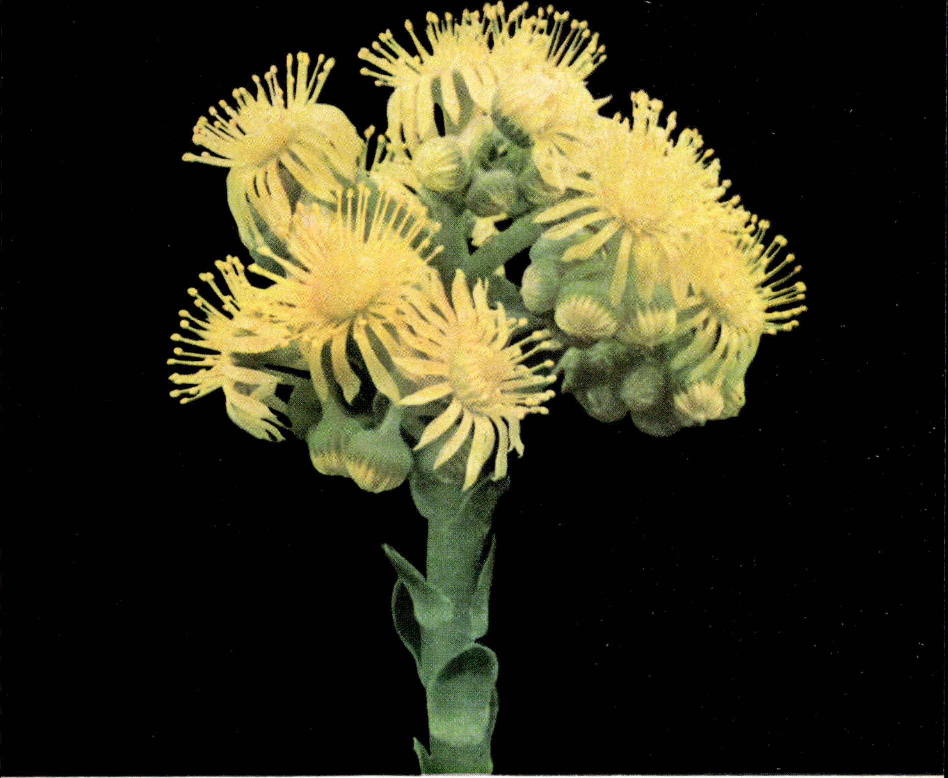

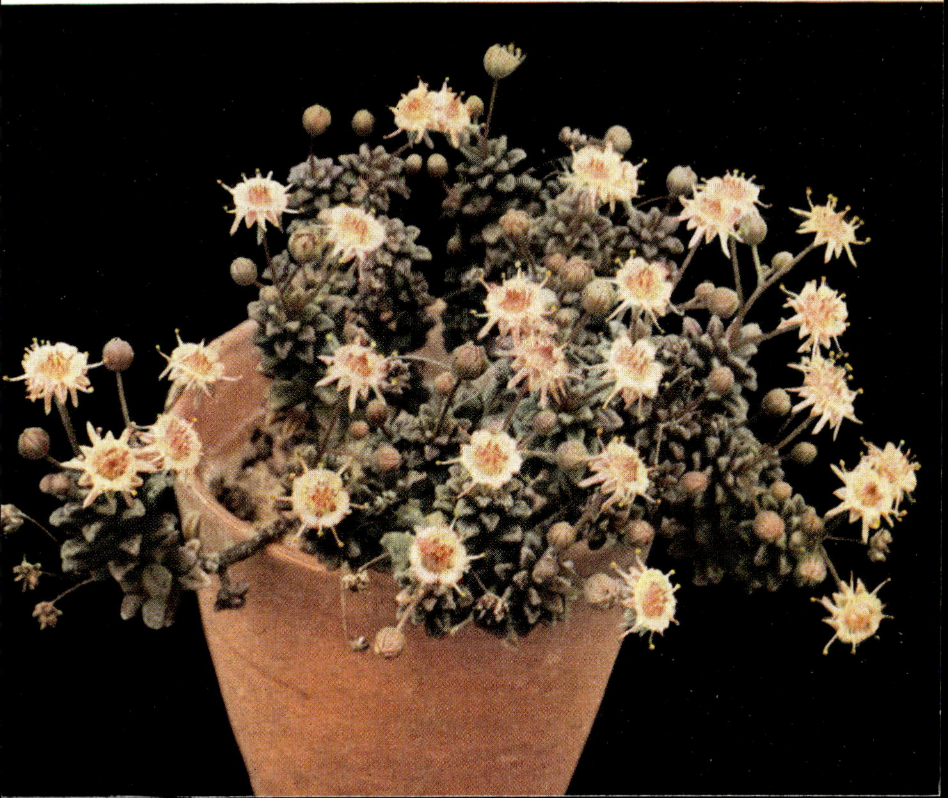

Monanthes adenoscepes *Svent.*
(Canary Islands)

COLOUR: Dull green hairy leaves, slightly streaked with purple.

SIZE: Rosette pictured is 1½ in. (3.8 cm) across.

FLOWER: Star-like creamy-pinkish, varying with amounts of sun.

NOTE: One of the newer dwarf *Monanthes*. Note the plant is " ringed " with what might appear as new branches, these becoming flower heads.

Well-drained soil, much less than average water, should be grown in slightly shady position and with slight winter warmth, when most water will be necessary.

Resting period in summer.

536

Monanthes niphophila   *Svent.*
(Canary Islands)

COLOUR: Dull blue-green with purple-black centre line to leaves.

SIZE: Shown at double natural size.

FLOWER: Star-like, brownish.

NOTE: Another more recently known species, dwarf in habit but possessing a deep " carrot-like " root.

Will stand long periods of drought if necessary, therefore well-drained soil is important and water rather below average at all times.

OXALIS

An additional genus, not illustrated in Volume I, is shown here as *Oxalis gigantea*, one of a number of succulent species coming from South America.

This genus in general is not difficult in any way under normal cultural conditions, providing the growing period for the particular species is watched and water is given accordingly.

Oxalis gigantea *Barn.*
(Chile)

COLOUR: Pale brown woody stems. Leaves bright green, very shiny and with velvety surface.

SIZE: Shown at half normal size.

FLOWER: Brilliant yellow.

NOTE: Not common in collections, this plant is without leaves during its resting period in summer when light spraying only is necessary. In autumn and onwards as growth appears, increase amount of water but keep in warmed greenhouse to allow proper growth.

A leafmould and sand soil suits the plant well and it is easy of culture in this way.

Oxalis gigantea *Barn.*
(Chile)

An enlarged photograph showing the velvety surfaced leaves.

NOTE: This plant displays " Nyctinastic movement," namely the folding up into a drooping position of the leaflets at night.

PELARGONIUM

The three species shown here depict the woody or almost trunk-like stem types as briefly referred to in Volume I, as can be seen from the three photographs I now illustrate, contrasting sharply with the trailing form of succulent *Pelargonium*.

Two species are illustrated in colour to show the flower differences.

Pelargonium echinatum *Curt.*
(S. and S.W. Africa)

See page 544 for Notes on this species.

Pelargonium ferulaceum *Willd.*
(S. and S.W. Africa)

See page 545 for Notes on this species.

Pelargonium echinatum *Curt.*
(S. and S.W. Africa)

COLOUR: Greenish brown stems, sometimes grey with brown-tipped
thorns. Leaves (when present) dull velvety green.

SIZE: Actual size of small plant pictured.

FLOWER: See colour illustration on page 542.

NOTE: One of the deciduous succulents, the resting period being in
summer, when usually it is without its leaves. During other months, this
species requires slight warmth, a rich soil and plenty of water, when its
many attractive flowers will be produced.

544

Pelargonium ferulaceum *Willd.*
(S. and S.W. Africa)

COLOUR: Grey, woody plant with dull velvety green leaves when present.

SIZE: Growing in a 4½-in. (11.4 cm) pot.

FLOWER: See colour illustration on page 542.

NOTE: Rarer in collections, also deciduous and resting, without leaves during the summer months. This is a much slower growing succulent *Pelargonium*, requiring much more open soil to ensure good drainage and less than average water.

Growing and flowering period autumn to spring. Winter warmth advised for best results.

Pelargonium paradoxum *Dtr.*
(Great Namaqualand)

COLOUR: Dull brown stems with pale green, slightly chalky surfaced leaves (when present).

SIZE: Slightly reduced.

NOTE: Yet another of the deciduous succulents of extremely slow growth, resting in summer when very slight spraying may be given.

As with others of this type, slight winter warmth, some water and a good but well-drained soil.

PEPEROMIA

Yet another genus, additional to Volume I, depicting the beautiful succulent form, the leaves of which when crushed smell strongly of aniseed, in the species illustrated.

Dwarf of nature, this genus appears to thrive in quite varied conditions, even including indoors as a house plant.

Peperomia nivalis *Miquel.*
(Peru)

COLOUR: Leaves bright green on upper surfaces, whitish to pink tinted beneath, undersides of leaves being roughened.

SIZE: Double natural size.

NOTE: This may be termed as being among the " windowed-succulents ", the upper part of each leaf having an opaque appearance.

Requires some water throughout the year and thus slight warmth in winter is necessary.

Slight shade suits it well, so indoor culture is also possible.

548

SARCOCAULON

A genus additional to Volume I, and of which all species are very slow-growing, similar in habit, and requiring almost identical treatment as given with the plant illustrated.

Flowers are usually solitary, varying between white and pink and having papery petals, five in number.

Sarcocaulon burmannii *Sweet.*
(Namaqualand)

COLOUR: Grey-brown stems and thorns. Leaves green.

SIZE: About natural size.

NOTE: Another very slow growing, deciduous succulent, the growing period being in winter and spring, often beginning during autumn.

Slight winter warmth, reasonable amounts of water, otherwise only slight in resting period when leaves will be absent.

SEDUM

The *Sedums* illustrated here differ very considerably from each other in general appearance and in temperature requirements—i.e. *Sedum dasyphyllum* which is among the completely hardy species which can be grown out-of-doors in the well-drained rockery in temperate climates.

Sedum palmeri is worth special mention as in general appearance it may easily be taken to be an *Aeonium*, as can be seen by comparison with several in the *Sempervivum* group.

Three colour photographs are included, along with three in half-tone.

Sedum dasyphyllum *L.*
(W. Europe)

COLOUR: Pale blue or slightly pinkish when grown slowly.

SIZE: Half size shown above.

FLOWER: White.

NOTE: One of the hardy species, suitable for pot or hardy rockery treatment.

A well-drained soil will keep this species even more compact than shown, especially when grown outside throughout the year.

If grown in the greenhouse in winter, a little water is necessary, even in cold weather. Flowering period—summer.

Sedum humifusum *Rose*
(Mexico)

COLOUR: Light green hairy stems.

SIZE: Slightly over twice its actual size.

NOTE: This very dwarf, prostrate-growing species is ideal for small pot culture when it will form into a compact mat-like growth.

Contrary to opinion of some people, this species will withstand much winter cold on an outside rockery, if protected from excess rain.

In the greenhouse, cold conditions are quite suitable.

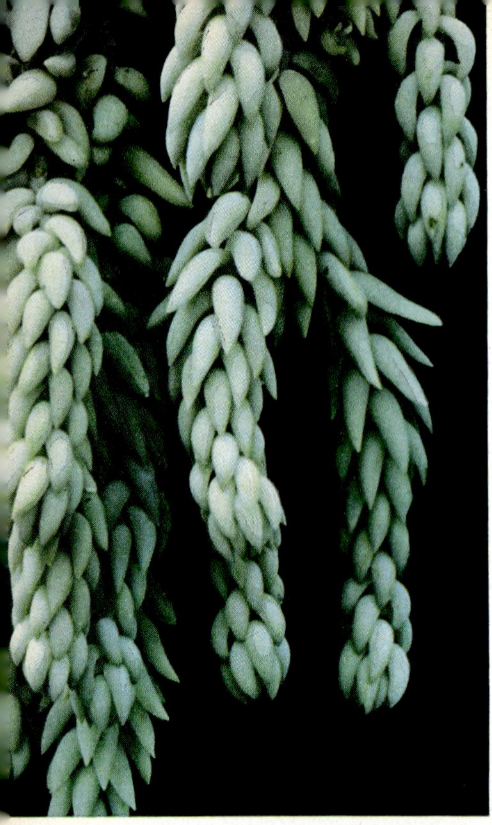
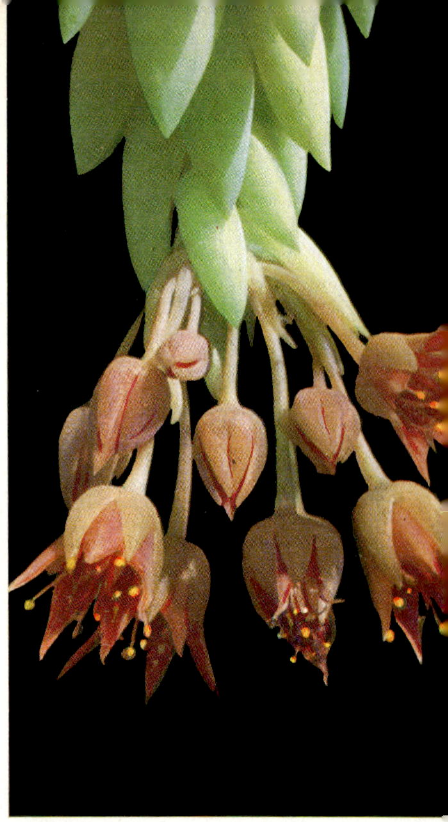
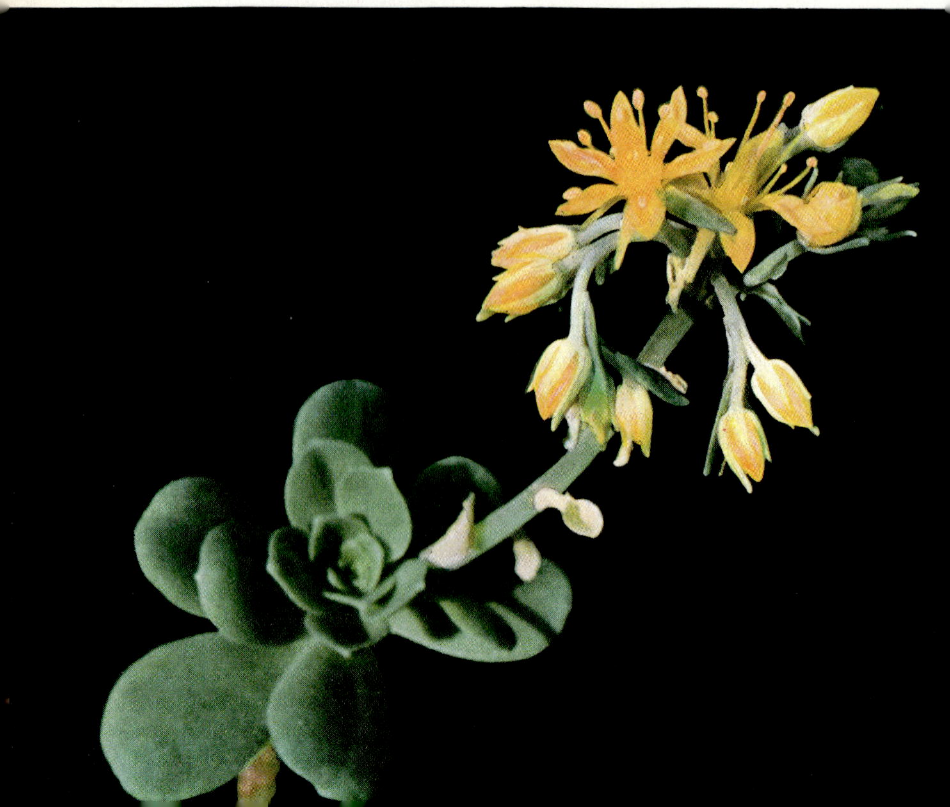

CV *These species belong to the* SEDUM GROUP

Sedum morganianum *Walther.*
(Mexico)

NOTE: A branching and hanging plant requiring plenty of water throughout the growing months. Soil should be very largely of leafmould for the finest results.

Flowers as shown in right-hand illustration usually appear in spring. An excellent plant for greenhouse or other decoration in a hanging-basket. Stands dry cold quite well.

CVI

Sedum palmeri *S. Wats.*
(Mexico)

NOTE: A very dwarf species, in appearance easily mistaken for an *Aeonium.*

The spread of leaves may be just over 1 in. (2·54 cm) across. Water with care at all times as it is a slow grower. Stands dry cold quite well in winter.

Sedum lineare fa. variegatum *Praeg.*
(Horticultural Origin)

COLOUR: Pale green leaves with a yellow variegated edge. Sometimes completely yellow branches may appear.

SIZE: Growing in a 3-in. (7·6 cm) pot.

NOTE: This beautiful *Sedum*, later of trailing habit; when large is particularly suited to the hanging basket.

A rich soil and plenty of water in warm weather, slight warmth and a little water being advised. Will stand cold if quite dry, but may lose many of its leaves.

SENECIO

Three half-tone photographs are included here to illustrate the varying forms to be found in this genus.

The flowers are not the principal attraction with these plants, but many varying and beautiful pastel shades of colour are to be found amongst the different species. Naturally, the intensity of light received by the plant plays an important part in the colour density.

Senecio crassissimus *Humber*
(Madagascar)

COLOUR: Chalky blue-green leaves with red edges.

SIZE: Shown slightly enlarged.

NOTE: Shown growing with a very distinctive leaf formation as will be seen by the photograph.

Slow in growth but liking a rich soil with some extra leafmould and plenty of water. Slight winter warmth necessary and a little water.

Senecio neohumbertii *Rowl.*
(Madagascar)

COLOUR: Greenish-blue leaves with a slightly chalky surface.

SIZE: Growing in a 5-in. (12·7 cm) pan.

NOTE: Not a fast-growing plant, requiring some winter warmth, when a little water can also be given. During growing season, rather under normal watering and a well-drained soil is important.

Flowering usually begins in late autumn.

Senecio oxyriaefolius *D.C.*

(Cape Province)

COLOUR: Bright green leaves with paler coloured veins. Leaf stalks green, streaked purple.

SIZE: Growing in a 3-in. (7·6 cm) pot.

NOTE: A curious *Senecio*, the growths coming from a much swollen root stock.

Likes plenty of water and some winter warmth, but if dry will withstand cold conditions, losing its leaves and stems completely, new growths being replaced again when conditions are favourable.

STAPELIA GROUP

This group was well illustrated in Volume I, and in addition these very fascinating succulents have been fully covered for the present in *Stapeliads in Cultivation*. In this book, I illustrated a good variety of species in both colour and half-tone photography, including several additional genera not illustrated in Volume I. These are: *Hoodia, Huerniopsis, Pectinaria, Piaranthus, Stapelianthus*, and *Tavaresia*.

This species belongs to the ECHEVERIA GROUP

Pachyphytum viride *Walther*
(Mexico)

See page 472 for Notes on this species.

This species belongs to the TRADESCANTIA GROUP

Tradescantia navicularis *Ortg.*
(N. Peru)

NOTE: Prostrate-growing, rather slow but requiring a wide pan in which to spread. Each branch or head of compact leaves measures barely 1 in. (2·54 cm) across, the upper surface of leaves being " windowed ".

Colour may vary according to intensity of sun.

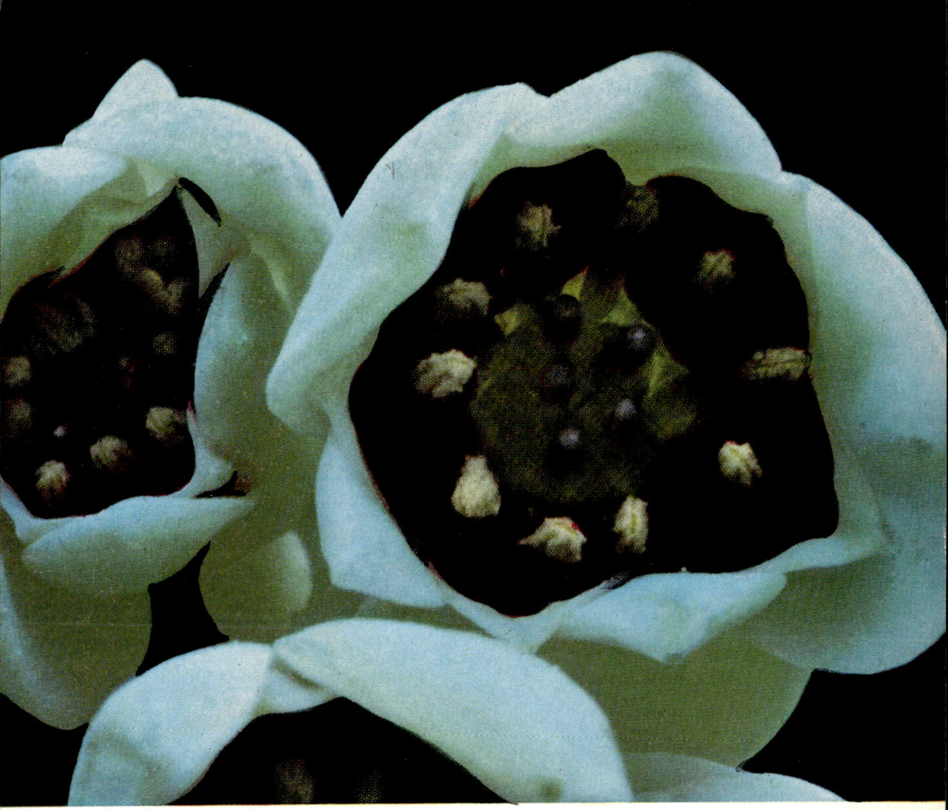

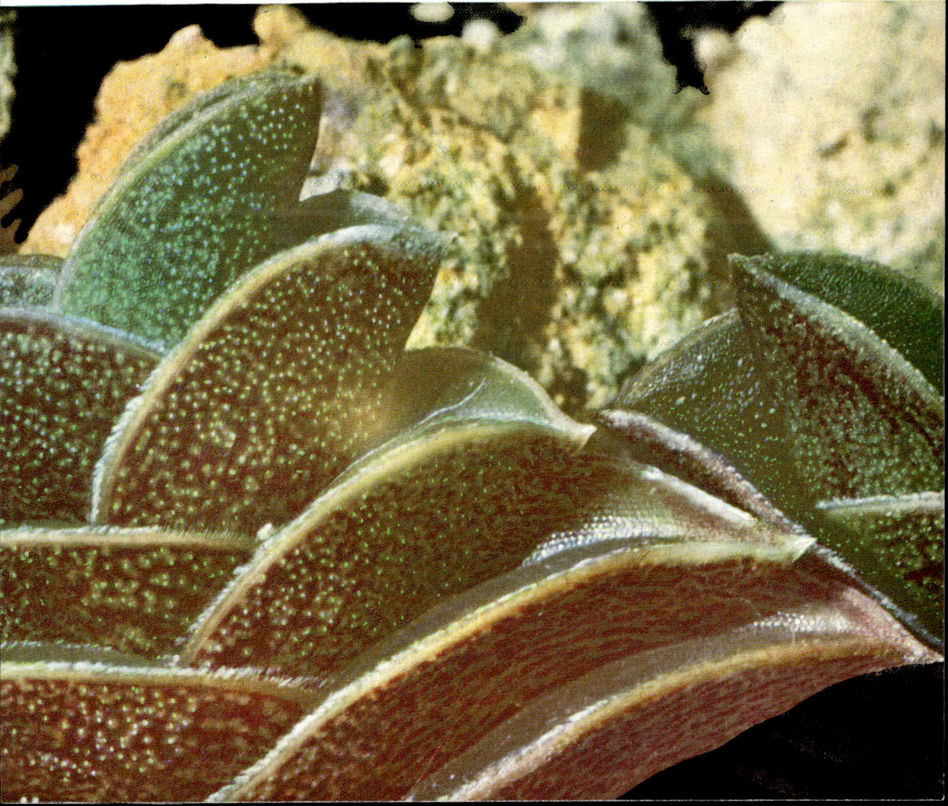

TESTUDINARIA

Commonly known as " The Elephant's Foot ", the bark-like swollen stem of which sits upon the ground, varying its patterns from plant to plant according to its speed of growth.

Many of these plants have been lost by collectors in the past due to observing too carefully the resting period and totally withholding all water. I have found that these interesting plants require some water throughout the so-called resting period, which is in fact when no leafy growth is present. Once the twining growths begin to appear from the centre, the growth of which is very rapid, the plants will require much water.

Healthy specimens, even if small, will develop a very large root system. If these roots are allowed to die through dryness, this is the cause of the failure.

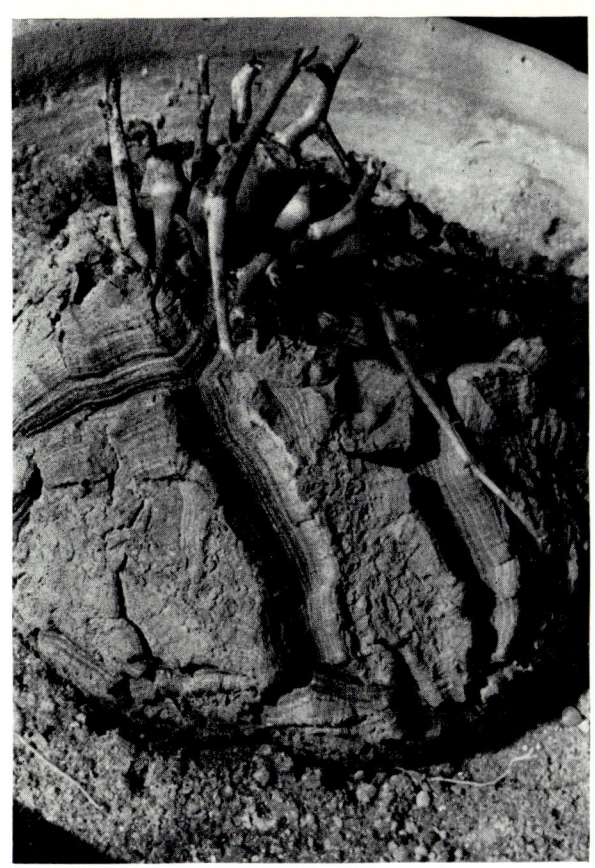

Testudinaria elephantipes *Salisb.*
(S. Africa)

COLOUR: Woody brown stem. Purple-green twining stems with shiny bright green leaves when present.

SIZE: Natural size shown.

NOTE: This is shown in the resting period which is usually in summer, when they require only slight watering or occasional spraying overhead. (Do not keep completely dry for too long.)

Towards autumn, very rapid growth of the twining stems will be noted; these later carry the leaves and flowers, some distance from the plant.

Water freely when in growth, but slight winter warmth is advised.

This species likes leafmould and sand only.

Testudinaria elephantipes *Salisb.*
(S. Africa)

COLOUR: (See page 565.)

SIZE: Shown twice the natural size.

FLOWER: (Not shown.) Fruit as photographed are green, edged with purple.

NOTE: This shows only a small section of the foliage with fruits.

A decorative species when in growth for training the foliage to any suitable positions. Flowers are small, greenish-white.

TRADESCANTIA

This quite well-known plant for its attractive leaf formation, namely *Tradescantia navicularis*, is one of the few succulent species and introduces one more additional genus not shown in Volume I. (see page 562).

Cultivation is quite easy as it can be grown in almost any reasonable conditions, standing dry cold quite well if necessary.

It is interesting to grow specimens in both shade and full sunlight and to compare them after a few months' growth. It will be found that the upper surfaces of each leaf will vary considerably in both colour and density of the " opaque " window to almost clear with the plant grown in shade.

APPENDIX B

GROWING IN MORE SOUTHERN LATITUDES

With the comparatively recent introduction of plastics, these materials have been found to lend themselves to various horticultural uses.

Of particular use to collectors living in more tropical climates, " Polythene " (Polyethylene), a plastic sheeting obtainable in long lengths and various thicknesses is worthy of special mention.

Collectors living in countries where very heavy rainfall occurs at certain seasons will find their succulents may often be lost through excess water, if unprotected in some way.

For outside rockeries of both cacti as well as other succulent plants, a light framework covered with " Polythene " can easily be erected just for the rainy season on corner posts in a sloping position. In this way a free airflow still exists, but heavy rain or hail is prevented from soaking or otherwise damaging the plants.

This material, although very strong and pliable, can be given added strength by placing it between two layers of wire-netting, such as chicken-wire of reasonably small mesh.

People to whom I have suggested this method report excellent results, despite severe hailstorms, frames standing up to such conditions for a season or so. As this material is cheap, its renewal after perhaps two or three years is advisable.

In addition to being a protection against rains, etc., this is also useful as slight shade protection in very hot sun.

THE
EXOTIC
COLLECTION

Part of the south end of the main house in which
the central area is planted-in. Plants vary in height
from a few inches to over 8 ft. (2·4 m) tall.

THE EXOTIC COLLECTION
Its Growth and Objectives

I have many times been asked to write something of the history of this unique collection from its beginnings over 25 years ago, to the present day when it is fairly described as " one of the most representative collections in the world ".

The objectives of any collector should be to grow successfully the plants of his choice, and to play his part in helping to preserve species which could very easily become extinct.

To every collector and enthusiast I would say: Do not be deterred from this aim because your collection may be small. I know greenhouse space is often limited, particularly in climates where winter calls for extra heating, but the small collector who grows and loves his or her plants is doing a big service to horticulture and can equally help to preserve the rarer species.

A number of features go to make it unique. Plants are grown under various conditions, their habits, health and flowering qualities being noted over the years. Not least in importance is any particular plant's resistance to cold or near cold winter conditions in the glasshouses. There is also the outside section for the study of the " hardy " species, some of which can stand very many degrees of frost without protection.

In the accompanying photographs it will be seen that parts of the collection form a " scenery-setting "—for instance, the Canary Island succulents have a small growing area of their own, as do some statley cacti from South America.

Stagings contain many species in pots or pans, as shown by the " *Echinocereus* staging " and the " *Mammillaria* staging ".

Variety is the essence of our present-day layout, which is constantly changing as new and more attractive ideas present themselves to house the ever-growing number of species.

Both colour and half-tone photography play a large part in recording the flowers, etc. Many readers will already be familiar with the Photographic Reference Plates which have been issued monthly for the past ten years, on an annual subscription. Every

571

Staging of *Mammillarias*, some of which are seen in flower. Many of these plants are of great age.

Part of the staging area of *Echinocerei*. Although not large plants, they are very fine flowering specimens.

photograph taken by me is from a plant in " The Exotic Collection ". This, of course, also applies to all the photographs of plants in this volume, and visitors to the collection can see the actual specimens illustrated; they can also compare the growth of the plants illustrated earlier.

EDGAR LAMB

Since the publication of this volume in 1959, many changes have occurred in " The Exotic Collection ", not least the wonderful growth of many of the actual plants illustrated in this book. Some of the views of the collection shown here have changed a great deal not only through the growth of the plants, but also through the addition of many new ones. When this volume was originally written the collection contained only some 4,000 different species of plants, whereas today it is well in excess of 9,000.

Needless to say, with this increase in the number of species in the collection, it has involved certain rearrangements within the present lay-out, so as to make full use of the space available, particularly as heating costs have to be borne in mind. Some additions to the growing area have been carried out, including a 70 ft. (23 metres) long house for S. American cacti, mainly belonging to the Cerei group, such as *Haageocerei, Oreocerei, Cephalocerei, Cleistocacti, Eulychnias,* etc. In fact, as this revised article on " The Exotic Collection " is being written we shall be starting the replanting of our entire *Mammillaria* collection, to name but one group, into their new home. A large new section has been added on to our main greenhouse, and it means that all the plants to be housed in this new part will be growing with free root-run, either in raised beds with a great depth of soil, OR in raised staging beds where the soil depth is only between 6 in. and 10 in. (15 cm–25 cm). It is in these latter beds that many of the smaller globular cacti such as the *Mammillarias* will be planted.

On page 572 in the lower illustration of *Echinocerei,* you will see that these plants were growing in pots, and these were in fact the first plants with which we experimented as to the advantages or disadvantages of free root-run in shallow raised beds. As a result of the fine results we have obtained from growing these actual *Echinocerei,* we have been gradually changing over other sections to this method. So those *Mammillarias* also shown on page 572 will also be transplanted, using this method. This does not mean that none of our plants will remain in pots, quite the contrary, some species or genera are best grown in pots for several seasons. Either they are very small plants and could easily be lost or become covered up by other quicker growing plants, or they are species requiring rather more care with watering, particularly in our climate, such that pot culture is safer. In addition as an important aspect of " The Exotic Collection " is the harvesting of " true to type " seed for distribution to our members later, it is sometimes easier to collect the fruits or seed pods from a pot plant rather than one growing in a rockery bed, etc.

To recap' slightly, we must mention that this collection has been in existence for well over 30 years, although it is only in the post-war years that it has become so widely known, partly through these books, but also through the monthly bulletins which are issued along with the photographic reference plates, all of which are now in colour. A number of features go to make it unique, as the plants about which we write are grown here under varying conditions for usually at least four to five years, before we go into print about them. This factor not only applies to the information in this book but also to the Exotic Collection monthly bulletin. In addition members are able to visit this fine collection by appointment, when many of them bring their cultural or identification problems for answering. This plant naming service to members may be by bringing the actual plant or sending in photos or colour transparencies.

Since the original publication of this volume, the large *Stapeliad* collection has continued to expand, as has so many other sections, not least the *Euphorbias* and *Aloes*, involving the addition of many of the rarer tropical African species, whilst we are also involved in a careful study of the *Echinocereus* genus, in an endeavour to simplify the nomenclature. One must realise that many plants in the past have been named either from single specimens or an isolated group of plants, without examining the many variations that do occur. We have gradually been collecting together live plant material of such and such a species from a wide range of habitats, sometimes separated from end to end on a map by 2,000 miles or more. It is only by doing this one can try to sort out where one species merges into another, which may eventually result in reducing the number of true species, and perhaps regrouping some species into just variety status.

EDGAR AND BRIAN LAMB*

---

* Since the original publication of this volume Mr. Edgar Lamb's son, Brian Lamb has joined him in " The Exotic Collection " and its more recent publications.

A rare *Aloe* in the foreground and behind—many fine
South American specimen plants. Also visible is
Euphorbia canariensis and two fine large plants of
Echinocactus grusonii.

Cleistocacti and *Haageocerei,* in the South American section of this house. Many of these flower well every year; their spine colouring is also most attractive.

A small area of succulents of the Canary Islands,
planted to best effect and as natural to habitat
as when collected in the wild.

577

Various cacti, etc., shown growing "wild" among rocky pathways. The tall cactus in foreground is a fine specimen of *Oreocereus celsianus*, with a very large specimen of *Euphorbia caput-medusae* to the left.

INDEX TO GENERA, VOLUMES I–V

(Species within each genus appear alphabetically)

	Vol. I	Vol. II	Vol. III	Vol. IV	Vol. V
	Page	Page	Page	Page	Page
Leuchtenbergia	—	—	655	—	—
Lithops	258	—	822	1132	—
Lobivia	85	371	628	953	1271
Lophocereus	74	—	—	—	—
Lophophora	111	—	—	—	1297
Luckhoffia	—	—	—	1191	—
Machaerocereus	—	353	—	—	—
Maihuenia	—	329	—	—	—
Malacocarpus (now *Wigginisia*)	112	—	660	981	—
Mamillopsis	—	404	—	—	—
Mammillaria	127	402	692	1016	1337
Manfreda	—	—	—	—	1409
Matucana	—	—	—	935	1251
Mediolobia (now *Rebutia*)	89	—	—	954	—
Melocactus	—	—	661	—	1318
Mila	—	—	662	—	—
Monadenium	—	494	—	1100	1444
Monanthes	—	536	—	1153	—
Monilaria	—	521	—	1144	—
Monvillea	—	—	610	—	—
Myrtillocactus	53	—	—	—	—
Nananthus	—	522	—	—	—
Neobesseya	—	—	—	1029	—
Neogomesia	—	—	—	982	—
Neohenricia	—	518	—	—	—
*Neolloydia*¹	—	—	—	1030	—
Neoporteria	—	—	666	983	—
Nopalxochia	156	—	—	—	—
Notocactus	113	—	659	990	1299
Nyctocereus	54	—	—	—	—
Obregonia	—	—	663	—	—
Ophthalmophyllum	—	527	824	1145	—
Opuntia	22	330	599	912	1229
Oreocereus	79	360	—	941	—
Oroya	—	—	—	—	1301
Othonna	—	—	842	1155	—
Oxalis	—	539	—	—	—
Pachycereus	55	—	—	—	1253
Pachycormus	—	—	—	—	1453
Pachyphytum	191	472	772	—	—
Pachypodium	—	—	847	1166	1487
Parodia	121	—	664	991	—
Pectinaria	—	—	878	—	—
Pediocactus	—	—	—	992	—
Pedilanthus	225	—	—	—	—
Pelargonium	274	554	—	—	—
Pelecyphora	—	404	—	—	1359
Peperomia	—	548	—	—	—
Pereskia	—	—	596	—	—
Pereskiopsis	—	—	—	—	1226
Pfeiffera	159	—	—	—	—
Phyllocactus	—	414	—	—	—
Piaranthus	—	—	879	—	—
Pilosocereus (see also *Cephalocereus*)	—	—	—	—	1265
Plectranthus	—	—	—	—	1478
Pleiospilos	—	527	827	—	—

	Vol. I	Vol. II	Vol. III	Vol. IV	Vol. V
	Page	Page	Page	Page	Page
Plumeria	—	—	—	—	1490
Porfiria	—	—	—	1032	—
Portulacaria	—	—	830	—	—
Psammophora	—	—	845	—	—
Pterocactus	—	338	—	—	—
Pyrrhocactus	—	—	665	—	—
Quiabentia	—	339	—	—	1228
Raphionacme	—	—	—	—	1449
Rathbunia	—	—	—	—	1255
Rebutia	90	368	630	957	1272
Rhinephyllum	—	518	—	—	—
Rhipsalidopsis	—	414	—	—	—
Rhipsalis	160	420	—	—	—
Rimaria	264	—	—	—	—
Rochea (now *Crassula*)	—	—	—	1076	—
Sansevieria	—	—	853	1173	—
Sarcocaulon	—	550	—	—	—
Sarcostemma	—	—	763	—	—
Sceletium	—	—	—	1146	—
Schlumbergera	—	418	—	—	—
Schwantesia	—	—	828	—	—
Scilla	—	—	—	1181	—
Sclerocactus	—	—	668	—	—
Sedum	277	552	—	1053	—
Selenicereus	—	354	—	—	1258
Senecio	279	558	—	1171	—
Solisia·	—	—	—	—	1361
Stapelia	294	—	880	1201	—
Stapelianthus	—	—	—	—	1494
Stenocactus	—	392	669	997	—
Stephanocereus	—	—	—	—	1267
Stetsonia	—	355	—	—	—
Strombocactus	—	377	—	—	—
Stultitia	—	—	—	—	1495
Sulcorebutia	—	—	—	—	1274
Synadenium	—	—	796	—	—
Tacinga	—	—	597	—	—
Tavaresia	—	—	—	1193	—
Testudinaria	—	565	—	—	·—
Thelocactus	—	—	672	—	1304
Thrixanthocereus	—	—	—	946	—
Toumeya	—	397	673	1001	—
Tradescantia	—	563	—	—	·—
Trichocaulon	306	—	877	1195	—
Trichocereus	56	—	—	939	—
Uebelmannia	—	—	—	—	1308
Utahia	—	—	674	—	—
Weingartia	110	—	—	1008	—
Werckleocereus	—	—	—	—	1259
Wigginsia (was *Malacocarpus*)	—	—	—	—	—
Wilcoxia	63	—	619	—	—
Xerosycios	—	—	884	—	—
Zygocactus (*Schlumbergera*)	155	—	712	1035	—

THE EXOTIC COLLECTION

Under the personal direction of   Letters to
EDGAR LAMB and BRIAN M. LAMB   16 Franklin Road,
                                         Worthing, Sussex,
                                         BN13 2PQ England.

EVERY MONTH, "The Exotic Collection" sends its members TWO NEW (previously unpublished) PHOTOGRAPHIC REFERENCE PLATES in COLOUR. (Size $8\frac{1}{2} \times 6$ inches), with non-technical cultural notes, etc.)

AN EIGHT-PAGE "Monthly Notes" (also illustrated in COLOUR). (A total for one year of 24 "Plates" and 96 pages of Monthly Notes—minimum = some 72 pages of *full colour*, plus articles and other cultural information. Some of these colour illustrations measure $11 \times 7\frac{1}{4}$ inches.)

SUBSCRIPTION also includes named seeds to member's own choice and plants are also available.

SUBSCRIPTIONS run from January to December each year—if you join during any year you will automatically receive all the back issues for the current year to the month of joining. After that future issues will be posted to you during the first week of each month.

SUBSCRIPTION for ONE YEAR
U.K. and Ireland   =   £4.50 (Sterling).

SUBSCRIPTION for ONE YEAR = $10.00 (U.S.A.) by sea mail.
                             $16.00 (U.S.A.) by air mail.